XXI CENTURY DICTATORSHIP IN BOLIVIA

XXI CENTURY DICTATORSHIP IN BOLIVIA

Carlos Sánchez Berzaín

Interamerican Institute for Democracy

Fondo Editorial

First English Edition

ISBN: 978-1505478099

Library of Congress Cataloging-in-Publication Data

Design: Kiko Arocha (www.alexlib.com)

Translated from Spanish by:
Edgar L. Terrazas, Traducciones LLC, ATA # 234680.

InterAmerican Institute for Democracy
2600 Douglas Rd, Suite 906,
Miami, FL 33134, U.S.A.
www.intdemocratic.org
Email: IID@intdemocratic.org

Editorial Fund from the
Interamerican Institute for Democracy

To those Bolivians who are persecuted, exiled, political prisoners and to their families. To the victims of the XXI century dictatorship in Bolivia.

Content

Foreword

Why are seminars and forums on democracy and Latin-American institutions now fashionable? Indeed, these have proliferated and; meetings, debates, and essays on the applicable concept of democracy in the case of Latin-America, continue proliferating.

The reason is that, as a novelty, what is at stake in the region's political system is the very concept of democracy itself.

There have been two twentieth century events that have changed the direction of the left (for that which this denomination can define). The first is the rediscovery of Antonio Gramsci by the intellectuals of the 70's, by the connivance of Argentinean exiles in Mexico with their local colleagues. The second is the creation of the Forum of Sao Paulo in 1994. There, under the helm of Fidel Castro, the subversive left decided that their ways would no longer be the use of armed struggle, but the electoral systems, especially in the areas of ideology and culture as these were promoted by Gramsci.

And thus, governments that could be considered as leftist emerged in Chile, Brazil, and Uruguay, amongst others. This opening also meant respect toward the institutions and the acceptance of certain conducts—on the economic side—that were unique to a liberal system; opening up to the rest of the world, respecting the laws of the free market, etc. One, of course, could disagree with the policies of these governments, but from a political perspective and not from an institutional one.

But a group of countries chose a different path, a path closest resembling a popular revolution, a path which a government normally achieves through elections. These are the ones that belong to the so-called "XXI Century's socialism" the brainchild of Heinz Dietrich, adopted by Hugo Chavez and supported by Havana's regime.

"Democracy's" firebrand no longer allows for anti-democratic regimes to exist; these were unthinkable by the end of the XX Century. This is why, what this is about, is to impose a limited resemblance of democracy, as a rudimentary concept that only considers popular elections, while setting aside all the other institutions that comprise the true meaning of a democratic system, such as; the reciprocal balance and control of powers, the independence of the judicial power and its constitutional control as an effective expression of the constitution's existence, the freedom of expression and its associated freedom of the press, and above it all, the rotational nature of those in power, through free, periodic and transparent elections. Without any of these features, democracy is not possible.

A characteristic of these types of governments is their populist nature. According to their own description, described by its mentors, such as; Ernesto LaClau, and Chantal Mouffe, this condition requires, unavoidably, a populist leader who heads the founding revolution, pretty much as, and similar to, the old dictatorial systems.

The concept of rotation in power is merciless upon the concept of chieftainship; the revolution aims to stay in power, not to deliver the power once the term for which it was elected has ended. Along these same lines, this revolutionary power must be concentrated in one person and its popular followership is maintained through a discourse which pretends to legitimize it, reinterpreting the past and projecting a distorted present. Under these conditions, there is no separation of powers, freedom of expression, and rotation in power, as mandated by the constitutions.

These are the reasons that lead their chieftains to disregard existing institutions, reform under any and all circumstances the constitutions to be able to decree the possibility of indefinite reelections and perpetuate themselves in power, all the while national assemblies are transformed into nominal agencies that are limited to sanction the whims of what the chieftain wants. The next step is, of course, the submission of the justice system, an action which consolidates this regime and one in which there are no individual rights or guarantees or the rule of law.

It is not only a problem of terminology, the perennial source of conceptual conflict. Whether we are talking about a republic, a democracy, an open society, the difference between the two systems is so obvious that it makes it overwhelmingly clear that it isn't just different words, under these conditions, there is no democracy.

The significant finding by a group of intellectuals and political experts is to have noted that in those countries where there are no institutions, what these are about are dictatorships, and that those dictatorships—because they had originated through popular elections and are fighting for their preservation from the inside—are remarkably different from the classical military dictatorships of the XIX and XX centuries. That group (Oswaldo Hurtado, Carlos Sanchez Berzain, Asdrubal Aguiar, Allan Brewer Carias, and others) have provided a clarifying feature to such situation, by calling its nature as "XXI Century's Dictatorships".

Just as Mr. Hurtado had dissected the case of Ecuador and Mr. Aguiar had scrutinized the case of Venezuela, the case of Bolivia was still pending, and is something that we now hear from Mr. Sanchez Berzain, former Minister of the Presidency (amongst other positions), attorney, and political scientist, and a victim of persecution by Evo Morales.

This work includes a broad view of his country's current situation and highlights the absence of the most minimum conditions of a republic's system and, moreover, reveals the previous circumstances that enabled Morales to access the power he enjoys that is as illegitimate as its illegal use itself.

The republic's requirements in order for a majority to be democratic and that to which we are now referring to, has been acknowledged for many centuries. This was enunciated by thinkers such as; Locke, Hume, Stuart Mill, Montesquieu, and was consistently reflected in debates aimed at ratifying the constitution of the United States, a true model of a government conceived as limited for the sake of the defense of individual liberties.

Sanchez Berzain, however, prefers to voice his defense of these concepts using the Inter-American Democratic Charter, to which he permanently refers to when he advocates for a democratic system. This method, perhaps, has the virtue of abiding to the letter of such charter, to a positive example of the state of law, since it is such charter—signed by all member countries of the Organization of American States—that by its binding nature sets aside a much weaker doctrinal discussion. I agree with him on the importance of the charter in this open conflict between those who are democratic and those who no longer are.

The appraisal of this OAS document is made in spite of the continuous misrepresentation of its terms by the Organization's General Secretariat, who has invoked it only to defend governments (in reality, the executive branch of such governments) when the other branches have attempted to defend constitutional principles, such in the case of Honduras and Paraguay. To the contrary, it has kept a silence verging on the absurd, in complicity with the flagrant violations to the terms of the Charter, such as what happened and happens on a regular basis today in Venezuela, Ecuador, Nicaragua, and Bolivia. If the "judgment of residency" that governed the Hispanic colonial America were still around, Insulza's future would not be coveted.

I met Carlos Sanchez Berzain when I was directing the Master's Degree Program in Political Sciences at FLASCO and Florida International University, from where he graduated with honors. He enrolled with the intent of refreshing his theoretical knowledge, forced by the exile to which the Bolivian dictator and the absence of independent justice in his country, had forced him into.

I believe that fact has enabled him to add to his extensive active political experience a capability for academic reflection that will benefit him whenever he goes back to the democratic Bolivia we all yearn to have.

Guillermo Lousteau
Miami, October of 2013

CHAPTER 1

Democracy in the Americas

1.1. Democracy: The basis of the Interamerican system

In the study and analysis of democracy we can find several definitions and concepts. These are; from those formulated in response to very honest academic concerns, to those others with an evident interest and political bias, aimed at justifying a position or the weakening or the elimination of democracy itself.

In this book we assume as a theoretical framework the description and formulation of what Democracy is in the Americas.

Democracy has been enunciated, proclaimed and declared as a fundamental principle in the organization of America's nations, and their international relationships. Democracy is evident in the birthing itself of the Organization of American States (OAS). The foreword of the OAS

Charter establishes that "...representative democracy is indispensable for the stability, peace, and development of the region."[1]

Along those lines we can affirm that democracy is the cornerstone of the activities of the governments of the Americas and hence of the Inter-American system. This so called democratic clause was established at the same time of the OAS' founding.

It was the transitional government of Peru, under the leadership of President Valentin Paniagua, who at that time while confronting a political crisis and democratic recovery, in April of 2001, made the initial proposal for the elaboration of an Inter-American Democratic Charter, right before the Third Summit of the Americas.[2] With this background, the Summit celebrated in Quebec from 20 to 22 April of 2001, adopted the so called "Declaration of Quebec" that institutionalized the democratic clause as the cornerstone of democracy in the region by establishing that "...any unconstitutional alteration or interruption of the democratic order in a state of the Hemisphere constitutes an insurmountable obstacle to the participation of that state's government in the Summits of the Americas process."[3]

---

1. Letter from Bogota, Bogota 1948, Documents of the OAS

2. OAS Documents. Evolution of the Charter.

3. OAS. Declaration of Quebec, Canada 2001.

The Inter-American Democratic Charter, upholding the importance of the democratic clause, was approved and signed[4] in Lima, Peru on the 11th of September of 2001 by all member countries of the hemisphere with the exception of Cuba (under Castro's dictatorship).

The charter gathers the doctrine, the observations, the history, the experience and the concepts of democracy from each one of the signatory American States. It currently constitutes the main source of international law and the source of internal standards of law, in each one of the signatory countries and it is, therefore, binding in nature.

1.2 The Interamerican Democratic Charter

The introduction of the Interamerican Democratic Charter acknowledges that "...democracy is indispensable, for the stability, peace, and development in the region." It reminds everyone that "the American Declaration of man's Rights and Duties and the American Convention on Human Rights contain the values and principles of freedom, equality, and social justice, that are intrinsic to Democracy." And it adds that "...the progressive development of international law and the advisability of clarifying the provisions set forth in the OAS Charter and related basic instruments

---

4. OAS Interamerican Democratic Charter

on the preservation and defense of democratic institutions, according to established practice..."

The legal instrument that provides answers to the question "What is Democracy in the Americas? is the Inter-American Democratic Charter. It does so, not through a mere definition but its description of democracy, it presents democracy in an undoubtedly wholesome and total manner."[5]

As stated by Ambassador Humberto de la Calle Lombana, who had presided over the Charter's working group and the negotiations that led the submitted text to be considered by the Assembly in Lima, "The Charter is a milestone in the democratic history of the hemisphere." First, from a political perspective, as it implies a serious commitment of governments to democracy, not only in its watered down version focused solely on the electoral processes, but as a wholesome concept that touches upon every aspect of human dignity as the main axis of its conception. Historically, it captures and projects its background that has served it as a guide, starting with the writings of the text itself all the way to the overtures related to the commitment from Santiago. Sociologically, the charter expresses a profound reality: The nations of the Americas believe they have the right to democracy, although there are some who believe that "their" democracy has not contributed, momentarily,

5. OAS Interamerican Democratic Charter. Documents and Interpretations, Washington D.C. 2003, p. viii.

to solve the many existing problems. Lastly, from a legal perspective, even though we are dealing with a Declaration and not a Treaty, it is clear that this isn't just any declaration since it was made as a means to update and better interpret the OAS founding charter, within the spirit of progressive development of international law.

1.3 Democracy

The Interamerican Democratic Charter in its first chapter, under the heading of "Democracy and the Interamerican System" defines what constitutes democracy on the basis of six aspects: Democracy as a right of the peoples of the Americas and as a fundamental factor for their development; the effective practice of democracy as a basis for the Rule of Law; the essential elements of democracy; the fundamental components of the exercise of democracy and the Rule of Law; the strengthening of political parties and other political organizations; and the citizens' participation.

The text of the first six articles of the Interamerican Democratic Charter contain, in summary, what the Governments of the Americas have conceptualized and accept as democracy:

Democracy as a right of the peoples of the Americas and as a fundamental factor for their development:

Article 1. The peoples of the Americas have a right to democracy and their governments have an obligation to promote and defend it.

Democracy is essential for the social, political, and economic development of the peoples of the Americas.

The effective practice of democracy as a basis for the Rule of Law:

Article 2. The effective exercise of representative democracy is the basis for the rule of law and of the constitutional regimes of the member states of the Organization of American States. Representative democracy is strengthened and deepened by permanent, ethical, and responsible participation of the citizenry within a legal framework conforming to the respective constitutional order.

The essential elements of democracy:

Article 3. Essential elements of representative democracy include, inter alia, respect for human rights and fundamental freedoms, access to and the exercise of power in accordance with the rule of law, the holding of periodic, free, and fair elections based on secret balloting and universal suffrage as an expression of the sovereignty of the people, the pluralistic system of political parties and organizations, and the separation of powers and independence of the branches of government.

The fundamental components of the exercise of democracy and the Rule of Law:

Article 4. Essential components of the exercise of representative democracy are; transparency in government activities, probity, responsible public administration on the part of governments, respect for social rights, and freedom of expression and of the press.

The constitutional subordination of all state institutions to the legally constituted civilian authority and respect for the rule of law on the part of all institutions and sectors of society are equally essential to democracy.

The strengthening of political parties and other political organizations:

Article 5. The strengthening of political parties and other political organizations is a priority for democracy. Special attention will be paid to the problems associated with the high cost of election campaigns and the establishment of a balanced and transparent system for their financing.

The citizenry's participation:

Article 6. It is the right and responsibility of all citizens to participate in decisions relating to their own development. This is also a necessary condition for the full and effective exercise of democracy. Promoting and fostering diverse forms of participation strengthens democracy.

1.4 The Essential Elements of Democracy

All of the features of democracy listed in the first chapter of the Interamerican Democratic Charter are important and reveal as to what democracy is in the Americas. The third article that refers to the essential elements of democracy, however, is wherein the fundamental crux of the matter lies.

Essential is what makes the essence, it is that which embodies the nature of things, that which is permanent and immutable in them, that which is most important and is inbred. Without the essential, the thing stops being as such because its nature is its characteristic property.

If we talk about the essential elements of democracy, we are in fact talking about the parts that constitute its nature itself, about its characteristic properties, about that which cannot be missing for there to be democracy.

When these elements are countless—such as in this case— we are dealing with the fact that the absence of just one of such essential elements renders as a result the inexistence of democracy.

The drafting of the Democratic Charter establishes, amongst others, five of these essential elements:

1.4.1. Respect for Human Rights and Fundamental Freedoms

Human Rights can be defined as "the intrinsic conditions that enable a person to be fulfilled"[6] and are inherent in all human beings without regard of any distinction or discrimination of any type.

Although the concept of human rights existed before the United Nations did, it is the rights expressed in the United Nations Universal Declaration of Human Rights[7] that gave it their institutional start and acknowledgement to have; universality, interdependence and indivisibleness, equality and non-discrimination, as properties, and highlight the fact that these human rights come with rights and obligations from those who are bestowed with, or are responsible for, them.[8]

In the Interamerican context, it is the American Declaration of the Rights and Obligations of Man[9] that acknowledges the right to; life, liberty, security and the person's safety, the right to equality in the eyes of the law, the right to religious freedom, the right to have freedom to investigate, freedom of opinion, expression, and broadcast, the right to the protection of one's honor, the personal reputation, and the private and family life, the right to the constitution and to the protection of one's family, the right to the protection of motherhood and

6. Hernandez Gomez, José Ricardo, Constitutional Law Treatise, Ariadna Editorial, 2010

7. UN Universal Declaration of Human Rights, Resolution 217A (III), December 10, 1948.

8. UN Universal Values, Department of Public Affairs, 2012.

9. IX International American Conference, Bogota, Colombia, 1948.

the infants, the right to live anywhere and to travel, the right to the inviolability of one's home, the right to the inviolability and circulation of correspondence, the right to the preservation of one's health and welfare, the right to education, the right to the benefits of one's culture, the right to work and fair wages, the right to rest and its enjoyment, the right to social security, the right to civil rights and the acknowledgement of legally standing organization, the right to justice, the right of citizenship, the right to vote and of participation in the government, the right of assembly, the right of association, the right to property, the right of petition, the right to protection against arbitrary arrest, the right to regular due process, the right to seek asylum, and the reach of the rights of man.

Human rights are in permanent evolution and currently these can be categorized[10] as rights of; first, second, and third generation.

First generation rights are those civil and political rights. These are the first rights legally consecrated that acknowledge every person to have:

- Fundamental rights and liberties without any distinction of race, gender, color, language, and social or economic position.
- The right to life, liberty, and legal certainty
- No one will be subjected to slavery or servitude

10.http://www.cubaencuentro.com/derechos-humanos/clasificacion-y-caracteristicas/clasificacion.

- No one shall be subjected to torture, or punishment or treatment that is cruel, inhumane, or degrading. No one will be physically, psychologically, or morally harmed.
- No one can be arbitrarily harassed in his/her private, family, domicile, or in his/her correspondence, nor suffer attacks against his/her honor and reputation.
- The right to freely move/travel and elect where to reside.
- The right to a citizenship
- In case of political persecution, every person has the right to seek asylum and to enjoy it, in any country.
- The right of men and women to marry and to decide the number of children they wish to have.
- The right to the freedom of thought or of religion.
- The right to freedom of opinion and the expression of ideas.
- The right to the freedom of assembly and pacific association.

Second generation rights or economic, social, and cultural rights, are those that have as an objective to ensure the economic welfare, access to work, and the education and culture, and are those that proclaim that every person has:

- The right to social security and to reap the enjoyment of economic, social, and cultural rights.
- The right to work under equal and satisfactory conditions.
- The right to unionize for the defense of his/her interests.

- The right to an adequate level of quality of life that ensures it and his/her family the health, feeding, dress, and housing, medical care, and necessary social services.
- The right to physical and mental health.
- During maternity and infancy, every person has the right to special care and assistance.
- The right to an education in its different modalities.
- Basic and secondary education is compulsory and free of charge.

Third generation rights are those rights so called of the nations that address matters of a supra-national character, such as; the right to peace, and a healthy environment.

As far as the respect for human rights and for the fundamental liberties as an essential element of democracy, these include, as a minimum, the respect for the rights and liberties acknowledged by the United Nations and by the Organization of American States, since it is not possible to conceive democracy without the respect for life, security, and the dignity of the persons.

Democracy does not exist in a government that imposes any type of servitude; in a government in which torture, cruel and inhumane or degrading treatment is imposed; where equality in the eyes of the law is neither acknowledged nor practiced, where there are no guarantees for effective resources to protect before the law those persons whose fundamental rights are violated; in countries where there are people arbitrarily arrested, incarcerated, or exiled; in a country where there are no impartial courts of justice; where the presumption of innocence and the non-retroactivity of the law are not respected; in governments where the right to seek asylum is not acknowledged; where private property is violated and illegal seizures and appropriations are committed; where there is no respect for the freedom of the press or freedom of expression; where people are persecuted for exercising these freedoms; or where there is no respect for the right to work.[11]

The violation (infringement) of even just one of these rights, as a reiterated action from the government, makes the respect of human rights as an essential element of democracy, to disappear.

1.4.2. Access to power and its practice with due subordination to the Rule of Law.

The Rule of Law establishes that the power and authority of the government are limited by law. Under the Rule of Law there can be neither not one person, nor not one thing that is above the law; it is a government of laws. It is a government that abides by the laws and institutions.

For the United Nations, the concept of "Rule of Law, has a central place in the purpose of its organization. It refers to a principle of governance according to which all persons, institutions, and public and private entities, including the government itself, are subject to the laws that

---

11. Contents of the Universal Declaration of the Rights of Man, Articles 1 to 24.

are publicly promulgated, these are equally enforced, and are independently applied, besides being compatible with the international standards and principles of human rights. Moreover, these demand that measures be adopted to ensure the respect of the principles of the laws' primacy, equality in the eyes of the law, accountability before the law, equity in the application of the law, separation of the branches of government, participation in the decision making, legality not arbitrarily, and legal and procedural transparency."[12]

When the head of government gets power by violating, altering, manipulating, modifying, committing fraud, or not abiding in any way by the norms, laws, or institutions, he/she does so outside of the Rule of Law. The same thing happens—it remaining outside of the Rule of Law—the head of government who may have gotten power in accordance with the Rule of Law that is by respecting the laws and institutions, but who exercises his/her power by destroying, substituting, counterfeiting, the laws and institutions.

When in the use of power the head of government creates his/her own laws to benefit him/herself, the implanted system remains outside of the concept of the Rule of Law, since the "imposed laws" are not legitimate because they have the expressed intentionality to do away with the existing laws and institutions.

---

12. UN Security Council. Report from the General Secretary on the Rule of Law and Justice, 3 August 2004 (S/2004/616).

1.4.3. *The execution of periodic, free, just, elections based on the universal, secret ballot as the expression of the nation's sovereignty.*

The electoral process is the mechanism by which a citizen makes a political decision to elect his/her representatives and authorities. Elections have, as a fundamental element, the freedom to act, to perform, and to decide. Anything that violates the citizen's freedom is a violation of the nature of the process itself.

Elections by themselves are not democracy; they are the central axis of democracy. Without elections there is no democracy, but having elections only is not democracy.

Elections, as an essential element of democracy, must be free and fair, and furthermore, must be based on a universal secret ballot.

Voting is universal because all persons who have attained the legal age provided by law and without any other condition or discrimination based on race, gender, income, or education, must vote.

It is secret as a guarantee for the voter not to be pressured for the contents of his casted ballot. The secret condition of the ballot is a guarantee for the voter to express his real will freely, without threats and the fear for retaliation. The nation's sovereignty means that the supreme authority of the State rests in the population, which is to say in the voters.

Besides the individual and free exercise of the right to vote, what "periodic elections" ensure is the "rotation of power" that in politics means "the change of government" based on the temporary and transitory character of the elected officials who can only last a given, specific period of time and who cannot not perpetuate themselves in power.

1.4.4. The plural system of political parties and organizations. This component calls for the existence of a system of multiple political representations that channels the will of the people and enables all sectors of society to participate.

Political parties and organizations are setup to function in a democratic environment and are organized to gravitate in the politics of a State, facing reality based upon their ideological or programmatic positions. Their objective is to legally seek power by means of the people's backing or through ballots that are cast in elections.

Political parties are considered fundamental to structure the political support towards any given programs, or socio-economic interests and values, add choices for the citizenry, form governments, and establish political agreements in the legislative terrain.[13]

Political organizations are, rather, groupings and entities of a citizenry's nature that seek to structure some segment or area of the population, by having specific objectives for their political activities. Perhaps the most notable difference between political parties and organizations may be the ideological content

---

13. Politics Matters: Democracy and development in Latin America, Interamerican Development Bank, 2005, J.M. Payne p. 165.

of the parties, compared to the organization's cause for social, sectorial, regional, or any other type of social mobilization.

The political parties' representation, because it is ideological, may be considered more limited, compared to the cause for mobilization of the organizations. In every case, both forms will always represent a preference of the society, reason why it is fundamental to allow it to act and participate in other preferences, which justifies plurality.

Under the Rule of Law, besides being the means for political participation that the citizenry has, political parties and organizations are venues for the expression of political pluralism for the shaping of the popular will.

The concept of political parties and organizations, in this essential component of democracy, indicates that society can and must organize itself in a way that it wishes in order to participate in governmental matters, on the basis of pluralism as an expression of freedom. It is unthinkable of a democracy that does not allow or provide for the citizenry to freely gather and organize.

1.4.5. The separation and independence of the branches of the government

The separation and independence of the branches of the government is one of the fundamental principles of the Rule of Law and its existence as an essential component of democracy is further ratified and acknowledged in the Interamerican Democratic Charter.

Montesquieu introduces the topic of the separation of powers of the government, noting the difference between; the empowerment to legislate rights (legislative), the ordering of said rights (executive) and of correcting that which was legislated or ordered by others (judicial). This is the basis of Montesquieu's thinking referred to as the doctrine of the separation of powers and the structure of the government of a republic[14] that is, perhaps, undoubtedly his most acknowledged contribution.

Although, today, we think the power of Government to be only one and that it to be divided into agencies, the designation of the governmental branches is still the most widely used. The branches, agencies or—if you prefer—departments of the government must discharge their responsibilities with independence and with a reciprocal political and functional control. At no time the legislative, executive, and judicial branches (and the electoral agency that some constitutions have added as a fourth branch of government) cannot be subject to the control or be subordinated to one same individual, or to only one of these branches, generally the executive branch.

None of the branches of government can neither become superior, nor subordinate the others, reason why to keep them adequately functioning, democracy-driven institutions uses

---

14. Lousteau, Guillermo. Democracy and Control of Constitutionality. Interamerican Institute for Democracy 2009, Pg. 88.

the separation of powers through a system of "controls, checks, and balances" (controles, frenos y contra pesos).[15]

The subjugation or encroachment of one branch of government by another is neither possible, nor permitted, and neither is the accumulation of powers in only one branch of government, because—besides guaranteeing good governance—the reason for the separation and independence of powers is to protect the individual rights of the citizenry.[16]

---

15. Anglo-Saxon terms whose origin is attributed to Montesquieu.

16. Hidalgo, Enrique, ICAP, Argentina www.diputados.gov.ar

CHAPTER 2

Socialism's Dictatorships of the XXI Century

2.1. Dictatorship

The Royal Spanish Academy defines dictatorship as "the government that under exceptional conditions ignores a portion, however sizeable, of the Rule of Law to exercise authority in a country" and as "a government that imposes its authority violating existing legislation."[17]

In a democracy no one person or institution can be above the law, since democracy is expressed by the Rule of Law wherein the laws comprise the basis for institutionalism.

In a democracy it is the constitutional institutionalism which grants the system one of its most important features and characteristics which is the "predictability".

Predictability as an inherent part of a democracy, and therefore of the Rule of Law, means that matters related to the system itself are known ahead of time, that—institutionally—

---

17. Royal Spanish Academy. Spanish Language Dictionary, 222 Dec. 2001.

what will happen later on can be predicted or be known. This is the certainty which; the constitution, the laws, and the subjugation of the authorities to them, grants.

Predictability allows the constituency to know when there will be elections, how long an elected official will be elected for, when that person will leave the government, how they must discharge their responsibilities, what the limits to their power are, what their obligations are, what the procedures to challenge their actions are, how they can be held accountable for their actions, and in a nutshell, everything an elected official can or cannot do, and for how long.

The most important feature of the predictability principle is that the citizenry can be assured that either supporting or opposing the government, their freedoms and rights will not be tampered with, even when their worst enemy has the highest political mandate of their nation. Because of predictability, the population knows that good or bad governments have a time limit to leave the government.

Under dictatorial regimes the opposite of democracy happens. Instead of no one person or institution being above the law and the Rule of Law, under a dictatorship either an individual or a group of individuals have exceeded the law and have placed themselves above the law. They tamper with it, don't abide by it, change it, and configure it to their liking. Nothing is predictable. They mandate their whim, circumvent institutionalism, and go as far as creating their own so-called "legal" system that is neither legal, nor legitimate, because it is not aimed at respecting the freedoms and rights of the citizenry, of the population, but to remain indefinitely and arbitrarily in power. "Dictatorships shape the regime itself, those who are in powers in non-democratic regimes have supremacy over the regime, incarnate the regime, and convert the State as the executing instrument of the regime."[18]

The main task of a dictatorship is to keep itself in power indefinitely, to have the total control of the Government and the citizenry. One of the basic instruments used to reach such an objective is to promote the political inefficiency of the opposition, to eliminate it, or to create an either functional or simulated opposition that contributes to the appearance and can be used as a mean to disguise the dictatorship as a democracy.

Dictatorships can be authoritarian and totalitarian. "In an authoritarian dictatorship, the government protects itself and does not infringe social and political institutions. A totalitarian dictatorship in addition to the political control also has control over the economy, health, education, food, housing, justice, and media and information sectors, and legal cybernetic networks, including an impressive capability to mobilize the masses."[19]

---

18. Shiling, Julio. Dictatorships and their Paradigm. Eriginal Books, 2nd Edition, February 2013, Pg. 49.

19. Shiling, Julio, Ob. cit., Pg. 20.

2.2. Cuban dictatorship survives and expands.

After the crumbling of the Berlin Wall and the subsequent collapse of the Soviet Union (URSS) in 1991, the dictatorship of Fidel Castro in Cuba was left in such a dire financial situation that it had to endure their so called "special period", a period of severe economic crisis that affected the life and health of the Cuban population and the stability of the dictatorship.

The vanished Soviet Union (URSS) stopped sending fuel oil to Cuba and the consequences were immediate and devastating, having to import approximately a tenth portion of the oil fuel it used to receive from the URSS. Their estimated Gross Domestic Product (GDP) for 1990 was reduced by more than 35% for 1993.

The arrival of Hugo Chavez to the presidency of Venezuela in 1999 and his immediate agreements with the Cuban dictatorship meant in fact the end of the aforementioned "special period".

For Cuba, the union between Chavez and Castro meant an extraordinary economic assistance that enabled it to stabilize the deteriorated dictatorship of Fidel Castro at a time in which the world expected the fall of the dictatorship and the liberation of the Cuban people.

For Hugo Chavez, this alliance—that would grow and strengthen over time—resulted in political assistance, guidance on security and intelligence, and the elaboration of a political plan with a hemispheric scope that has enabled the growth of the influence and dominion of Castro's dictatorship, its ideas, and mechanisms that gave Hugo Chavez the leadership beyond the borders of his country.

Besides its economic rescue and the ending of the "special period". Castro's dictatorship could now recreate its penetration and expansion plans for the decade of the sixties. The ideology, the anti-democratic and anti-American methods of the island's government, coupled with the unlimited amounts of money and resources provided by Chavez from the Venezuelan oil wealth, allowed it—without notice from the democracies of the hemisphere—to implement a renewed project to intervene and control the Latin-American countries.

The first objective was the consolidation of Hugo Chavez's absolute power in Venezuela while, simultaneously, Cuban embassies and agents started to operate destabilizing mechanisms in Latin-American countries. Again—just as in the decades of the sixties—Bolivia, Peru, Ecuador in the Southern cone, Nicaragua, Honduras, El Salvador in Central America, were chosen as objectives for the expansion which would rapidly reach all Latin American states.

This is how the political expansion project was born in Latin-America. From Cuba's agonizing dictatorship—rescued and fueled by Chavez's Venezuelan money—targeting the democracies of the hemisphere that are always subjected to economic harshness and political uncertainties. Democracies which, at that juncture, were battling against a regional economic crisis, the internal social discontentment inherent of an economic crisis, and the pressure from multilateral economic organizations.

With the birth of this project, the political situation in the Americas started to change, eliminating the democracies of several countries to give way to the "dictatorships of the XXI century"[20] placing under this threat almost all democracies, subjugating almost all, starting a period of high social conflict in the region fueled by the political and economic support from the La Habana-Caracas axis, and getting to the point of controlling or conforming regional organizations of a political and economic nature.

In summary, the political landscape of the region is changed from a democratic America with an isolated dictatorship, to an America that reveres that dictatorship, with the expansion of this type of regimes to countries such as, Venezuela, Bolivia, Ecuador, and Nicaragua, and the rest of the nations permanently threatened with destabilization.

2.3. Bolivia: Violence to shatter democracy.

Bolivia had already been chosen as a priority objective for the expansion of Castro's project in the decade of the sixties through an armed focus that the Cuban dictatorship was able to put in place with the guerrillas commanded by Ernesto

---

20. Hurtado, Osvaldo, XXI Century Dictatorships. The Ecuadorean Case. Paraiso Editors, Quito, Ecuador, 2012.

Guevara. Shortly after taking power in 1959, Castro had started an expansion project into the Americas that would include the placement of rural guerrillas, urban guerrillas, terrorism, and open confrontations, in almost all of the countries of Latin-America.[21]

There are several reasons why Bolivia was always a priority target for the Castrist plans and was chosen as the first country for the project's expansion agreed between Hugo Chavez and Fidel Castro. Some of these reasons—similar to the ones in the sixties—were subsequently confessed and admitted by their authors and at the beginning of this century, were:

- The geographic location of Bolivia, because geo-politically it would enable the influence to spill over on the five countries that surround it (Argentina, Chile, Brazil, Paraguay, and Peru), and even on Uruguay.
- The fact that Bolivia was always considered a country that could be easily penetrated due to its historical political instability, poverty levels, social situation, etc.
- Because it was assessed by Cuban intelligence as a country "inexpensive for political-subversive operations", since the cost in Bolivia on matters of mobilization, confrontation, and destabilization actions, are far less than what would be in other countries.

---

21. Interamerican Institute for Democracy. Castrist influence in the Americas, Miami's Book Fair, 2011. www.intdemocratic.org.

- Because it has always had very combative social movements such as those from the miners and peasantry.
- Because since the ending of the eighties a very combative sector had been developed and mobilized, the Illicit Coca Leaf Growers, with lots of experience in the use of union's violence against the Government.
- Because when the plan elaborated in Habana with monies sent from Caracas was put in place, Bolivia was being governed by a former military dictator[22] who had gotten to power democratically, but who had a very weak government.

With these and other conditions unnoticed by the government and the opposition, the project to take over the government was put in place early on, for what we would later call XXI century socialism, or the ALBA Project. The first attacks were against the government of General Hugo Banzer Suarez and they are known as the "Altiplano Blockade" and "the War Over Water".

The year 2000 started in Bolivia with a set of conflicts that took the government to decree a State of Siege that could never be complied with and that, instead, spread out and generalized the conflict. A hunger strike by Bolivian policemen deteriorated into a mutiny; an anonymous document supposedly signed by members from the Armed Forces proclaimed their solidarity with the policemen; in the city

---

22. Hugo Banzer Suarez, democratically elected for the period 1997-2002.

of Cochabamba, peasant and coca growers took the city in protest to the rising of the water fees (The War Over Water).

A blockade of the highways decreed by the altiplano peasants cut the route to Peru and when the Army entered into the Achacachi community, two hours away from La Paz, the Aymara Peasants attacked them with firearms; a Captain was wounded and was taken to a local hospital from where the infuriated peasants took him and beat him to death. Under this conditions, the government was forced to concede to the policemen. It gave them a 50% raise in their salaries—they were asking for 30%—rescinded the contract with, Aguas del Tunari, the water provider in Cochabamba, and modified the law of waters... (sic)[23]

The government of General Banzer accused the opposition to have attempted to overthrow him and the opposition led by the National Revolutionary Movement (MNR) accused the government to be inept. Neither the opposition, nor the government, however, had taken notice then —and realized when it was too late—that what had happened at the start of 2000 was a field practice run that had not been able to overthrow the government. General Banzer was not overthrown, perhaps because the movement to do so was not coordinated and lacked leadership, and because with all the criticism made of his government, he was able to keep his government united, he did not endure or

---

23. The Altiplano in Flames, Semana.com, May 15, 2000.

controlled any internal betrayal, and conceded totally when he no longer had any other options. Banzer remained in power until 2001 when he was compelled, due to an illness that eventually caused his death, to delegate his mandate to his Vice-President Jorge Quiroga.

The year of Jorge Quiroga's government was not free from pressures, confrontations, deaths caused—as in all governments- by the Coca Growers' Union leader Morales. The most important thing—due in large part to the political fallout it generated- occurred in October of 2001 when the Coca Growers' Union leader Evo Morales directed the perpetration of violent acts in the area of Sacaba, Department of Cochabamba, that resulted in several fatalities and dozens of wounded. This situation prompted calls for his ouster from Congress where he was a representative, and for his criminal prosecution. Despite ample evidence, the decision by the then Minister of Government, Mr. Leopoldo Fernandez[24] to plea bargain with the mediation by the Catholic Archbishop from Cochabamba, kept Morales from being prosecuted and sent to jail, facts that Morales used as a fundamental part of his campaign for the 2002 elections.

The 2002 election was won by the candidate for the MNR, Gonzalo Sanchez de Lozada who forged a Governmental Coalition along with the Movement of the Revolutionary Left (MIR) of Jaime Paz Zamora, and the Civic

---

24. Afterwards Governor of the Department of Beni. Today a political prisoner of Evo Morales.

Solidarity Unit party (UCS) under the helm of Johnny Fernandez, son of the populist leader Max Fernandez. Economic crisis and rampant unemployment were the setting for the assumption of a weak government in a country in crisis, where the campaign sustained in the last few years against the so called "traditional" political parties and political leaders (similar to what had happened in Venezuela and what was happening in Ecuador, Nicaragua, and other countries), and now created a high risk backdrop.

The same day of the Presidential inauguration, the 6th of August of 2002, the leader of the Coca Growers Union, Evo Morales, called on Bolivians to "overthrow Sanchez de Lozada", while the President called the population to a national dialog to overcome the dire economic and social crisis with which he was assuming his mandate.

In January of 2003, Morales shifted to a more direct attack strategy, blockading the roadways in the Cochabamba area, actions that were defeated by the government and incomprehensively, at the request of the bishops from the Catholic church, Sanchez de Lozada saved Morales from a crushing defeat, and subscribed a person to person agreement.

Almost immediately thereafter, and using a tax increase as a banner—a tax increase had been promulgated by the government to keep the fiscal deficit in check (under pressure from its economic team and in-spite of its political team's opposition)—on the 12th and 13th of February of

2003, a policemen's strike and mutiny ensued that resulted in an armed attack against the Government's Palace where the President was. There was a confrontation between the mutineers and the military that defended the Presidential Palace, with the tragic results of 30 dead and several wounded and the attempted assassination of Sanchez de Lozada by shots directly aimed against him and his office. These acts were investigated by the Organization of American States who published its findings[25] in which it asserts that "the shots fired on 13 February against the Presidential Palace put the life of the President at risk" and that "the Army acted in defense of democracy and the Rule of Law when the police attack occurred" and recommended that "the fair and just solutions that are sought, in order to avoid the occurrence of events similar to those of 12 and 13 of February, must be found within the laws of the democratic system and only by applying solutions provided for in the Constitution ...and, in essence, that all actors of Bolivian public life make a commitment not to use violence to gain political objectives, and that they not depart from the Rule of Law to obtain their political or social revindications."[26]

It is a fact that the events of February of 2003, had been close to eliminating the President and the democratically elected government, and even though the OAS Report recom-

---

25. OAS, Report by the OAS on the facts of February of 2013 in Bolivia. General Secretariat May of 2003.

26. OAS, Report Feb 2003, Bolivia, cited.

mended impunity, no investigation against the perpetrators, accomplices, instigators, and authors, was ever conducted.

The New Republican Force (NFR) political party led by Manfred Reyes Villa[27] joined the governmental coalition and efforts to eliminate the government and democracy continued. The coca growers' (cocaleros) congressional representative Evo Morales began to openly and publicly travel to Venezuela to receive funding support from Hugo Chavez and, under the cloak of congressional immunity, he transported the funds back to Bolivia.

In August of 2003 the Military Attaché from the Venezuelan embassy in La Paz, was detained for conspiring and inducing others to conspire against Bolivian officers to whom he offered money for their support of civilian groups "who had been prepared" for acts against the government. President Sanchez de Lozada opted to resolve that situation through confidential diplomatic means, ousting the Attaché, filing a Diplomatic Complaint against the government of Chavez, with whom he spoke telephonically over the matter—and avoiding its dissemination through the media.

This same month of August the government opened a new national dialogue, with the mediation of the Catholic Church, which was suddenly and abruptly terminated when Evo Morales after having returned from one of his trips to

---

27. Currently exiled in the United States after having served as the elected Governor of Cochabamba and having ran as a Presidential candidate in 2009.

Caracas, announced to the bishops of La Paz that there would be no dialogue and that "a hard confrontation was forthcoming."[28]

With that backdrop of announced warfare, the so called "War of the Gas" was started which would ultimately end in the forced resignation of the constitutionally elected president. An alleged governmental decision to export gas to the United States through Chile was used. Not only had the government not made the decision, but had not even announced it.[29] The subversive operations were centered in La Paz where there were blockades of roadways, oil refineries, supply routes, seeking to isolate the seat of government.

In Sorata, a town that had just celebrated its anniversary on 14 September, the peasant mobilization kidnapped all national and foreign tourists that had attended this celebration and the government had to order a rescue operation to take place which enabled more than fifteen hundred unharmed people to return to La Paz, but that in their return were victims of an armed ambush directed by Felipe Quispe with the resulting death and wounding of several policemen, military, and peasants.

Quispe himself has confessed his participation in a press interview; "Once our comrades are already detained, I or-

28. Episcopal Conference. Bishops from La Paz and El Alto, in verbal communication with the Ministers of the Presidency and Defense.

29. Marquez, Nicolas. The Impostor. Contracorriente Editorial, Argentina, 2012, Pg. 74.

der the rank and file, some of the people who had received guerrilla training from the EGTK, to execute our strategy against the government. Moreover, I order them to take weapons to engage the military. Then, our people trained by the guerrillas, have ambushed the policemen with one dead and several wounded. That was the reason for the military to intervene Warisata."[30]

The overthrowing of the constitutionally elected government is acknowledged after the fact *(a posteriori)* as a political merit: "The Sole Confederation Union of Peasant Workers From Bolivia" (Confederación Sindical Única de Trabajadores Campesinos de Bolivia) - CSUTCB, takes credit for the political-military strategy and tactics of Tupac Katari, due to the fact that is still latent and intact in the soul and heart of the new indian. This is why, we entered into the political scenery with armed roadway blockades, shutting off agricultural products, conducting protest marches, hunger strikes, and the siege of colonial cities until we are able to strangle and kill of hunger the bourgeois q'aras" *(sic; q'ara is derogatory term referring to a person's Caucasian or Anglo-Saxon features and appearance).*[31]

The truth is that in order to promote violence, the armed attacks against; the population, government officials,

---

30. Opinion, (Daily Newspaper) Bolivia. The ambush to the police was to kill "The Fox", April 8, 2013.

31. Quispe Huanca, Felipe. The fall of Goni, Pachacuti Editions, July 2013, Pg. 9.

and public as well as private property, in the attacks that
started in August of 2003 and ended with the overthrowing
of President Sanchez de Lozada, in addition to the national
conspirators, others participated; Cuban agents and operators, Venezuelan military from the Chavez government,
FARC armed elements[32], peasants from Peru trained by
the EGTK[33], coca growers, and policemen that had been
involved in the February attacks. All in all, everything and
everyone that the Castro-Chavez alliance could muster, to
start and if necessary conduct, a civil war.

The bloodshed and confrontation had been planned for
the destabilization and had already happened even in previous democratic governments, but the resultant overthrow
of the President would have not, ever, occurred without the
concurrence of a political element that became a fundamental part of the conspiracy: The betrayal of the Vice-President Carlos D. Mesa Gisbert.

Mesa, guided by his economic ambition and thirst for
power in the midst of this crisis and attack against democracy, publicly announced what he called his "side stepping",
his distancing himself from the government and thus leaving open the way to the constitutional succession, so that
the coup d'état overthrow could be disguised as a resignation. "Mesa wanted to be President at all cost, at the start of

---

32. The New Herald, September 30, 2004, Pg 2B.

33. The New Herald, December 27, 2003, Pg 1B.

the 2002 campaign he had asked me –and even told Goni – that he (Mesa) should be the presidential candidate. In order to run as a Vice-presidential candidate he placed onerous conditions, in fact he bartered and sold his candidacy, to the point that the same day of the proclamation, Mesa continued negotiating economic conditions and concessions of power... in January of 2003 the national dialogue failed and Mesa proposed a project for Goni's orderly succession." During the crisis in September and October of 2003 "Mesa knew everything that was happening, he had approved and authorized it, because he participated in all of the meetings in which decisions had been made."[34]

The overthrow of President Sanchez de Lozada and the success of the coup d'état planned by the Latinamerican dictatorial current, was consummated on the 17th of October of 2003 with the forced signing of a resignation in which the President expressed: *"by placing my resignation under the consideration of the Honorable National Congress, I do so with the utmost conviction that it cannot be accepted because a President, who has been democratically elected, cannot be removed by mechanisms of pressure and violence that are on the fringes of the law."*[35]

The clarifications of facts that cost the lives of more than 60 Bolivian citizens, and left dozens of wounded, ended the

---

34. Lema, Gonzalo. The Bolivia that leaves, the Bolivia that comes, Los Tiempos, La Prensa, Bolivia, August 2011.

35. Sanchez de Lozada, Gonzalo. Message to the National Congress, October 17, 2003. See Annex 3.

government of Sanchez de Lozada and are a milestone for the end of democracy in Bolivia, and are, undoubtedly, a pending situation. These facts, up to now, have only served to attack the so called "traditional" political class, persecute, jail, or force into exile political leaders, military, public servants, and citizens who defended democracy, the Constitution, and the laws of the Republic.

Carlos Mesa got to the presidency as a successor of the overthrown President Gonzalo Sanchez de Lozada who had been constitutionally elected. He assumed power in political chicanery with the over-throwers and connived with them in the so called "October's agenda" as Mesa himself acknowledges and publicizes on his Web page: "The day after being sworn in, Mesa delivered a speech to the mobilized sectors in the city of La Paz, promising to: 1) Have a binding referendum over the gas, 2) establish a Constituent Assembly, and 3) a reform to the Law of Fossil (hydrocarbon) Fuels, that would include the reviewing of the privatization procedures and processes,"[36] to which a few days after were added the "prosecution proceedings against Sanchez de Lozada and his collaborators."

The October's Agenda is nothing else but an agenda for the start of the dismantling of the democratic institutions in Bolivia, and is the direct result of the previous covenant that Mesa entered into during the conspiracy process which

36. http://carlosdmesa.com/2013/02/07/el-referendo-sobre-hidrocarbu-ros-referendum-del-gas-de-18-de-julio-de-2004/

he took part in and of which he was the first to benefit from. This is why, before he completed his first two weeks as the President, he signed an "amnesty"[37] to benefit his accomplices, to exclude them from any type of investigation and prosecution. Carlos Mesa issued Supreme Decree 27237 that grants amnesty to all social actors of October of 2003 (thus releasing them from any liability to be prosecuted those who caused the crisis, with Evo Morales among them). The decree was amended afterwards to specify that the amnesty did not apply to former members of the Government, but only to the social movements."[38]

Evo Morales, personally, started, promoted, and continues to promote the prosecution solely against those overthrown, directing an investigation only against members from the deposed government, accusing them of the dead and wounded that Morales himself, along with Quispe and foreign agents and their accomplices caused in their conspirator actions and other acts of violence.

With Sanchez de Lozada overthrown, Bolivia's democracy was fatally wounded. Conspirators were intent to seek the quick application of October's Agenda to break down the institutional defenses that the Constitution had.

Mesa's allies of October 2003, themselves, placed him under successive pressure, forcing him to resign "after as-

37. Mesa Gisbert Carlos D. Supreme Decree 27234, 31 October of 2003.

38. Supreme Decree 27237, 4 November of 2003 http://es.wikipedia.org/wiki/Guerra_del_Gas (Bolivia), Conflict and Death.

suring everyone that Bolivia was at one of its most difficult times in its history. According to Mesa, the time had arrived in which none of the laws are abided, and it was a time in which a few were forcing their will upon the rest of the population."[39] Surely, the twenty months of government, following his betrayal, made Carlos D. Mesa forget that he himself has taken the democratically elected government of Gonzalo Sanchez de Lozada, to that situation. What was happening to Mesa was but the predictable result of his actions. Moreover, not even one citizen had voted for Carlos Mesa to be President.

So, Mesa left the presidency on the 10th of June of 2005 and the National Congress designated in his place the Chief Justice of the Bolivian Supreme Court Eduardo Rodriguez, so that within a deadline of six months, he would call for and hold general elections.

The elections were won by the Cocalero (Coca Growers) leader Evo Morales. He did it over the discredit of the country's democratic political system and with the backing of the entire economic and publicity apparatus of his sponsors from Caracas and La Habana. Once Evo Morales was sworn in as President, the only thing left to do was to follow the same path that had been threaded by Chavez in Venezuela to complete the institution of Socialism's XXI Century dictatorship in Bolivia.

---

39. El Mundo.es. The country is crumbling apart, June 7, 2005.

CHAPTER 3

Undoing the Country's Constitution

3.1. The constitutional counterfeiting

With Evo Morales in power, the objective in Bolivia, set by the foreign controllers was to eliminate the democratic institutionalism and substitute it for a system of their own that would preserve the image of being democratic. In order to do this, the model to be guided by was that of Venezuela, since Chavez had made important strides in the institutional dismantling of his country.

The main pitfall was the Constitution of the Republic of Bolivia. Applying "October's Agenda" Carlos Mesa advanced an unconstitutional proposal that was promulgated on the 20th of February of 2004, to reform the existing Constitution and to include as a mechanism for deliberation and government of the people a Constituent Assembly, the citizenry's initiative, and the *referendum*. It created the Coordination Unit for the

Constituent Assembly (UCAC) that set the organizational basis for the convocation that would take place in 2006.

Mesa promulgated the constitutional reforms declaring that these "would allow the convening of a constituent assembly that would open the path to a new social covenant to safeguard democracy", adding that "the 15 reforms introduced to the Basic Charter are part of the historical transition started with October's bloody popular revolt and that must conclude with the profound transformation of the Government."[40]

What the so called constitutional reform of 2004 actually did, however, was to introduce a mechanism through which the constitution would be annihilated by inserting, without the legal basis to do so, the "total reform of the constitution" by means of the constituent assembly that did not exist in the original fundamental charter of the Republic. The new institution, which in and by itself is counterfeit was drafted this way:

Article 232. The total reform of the Constitution is the exclusive jurisdiction of the Constituent Assembly, which shall be convened by a Special Convening Law, that will establish the forms and modalities for the election of constituents, will be ratified by two thirds of the votes of members present of the Honorable National Congress, and will not vetoed by the President of the Republic.[41]

---

40. A.P. Bolivia, La Paz, February 20, 2004.

41. Bolivia. Law 2631 of February 20, 2004.

Neither the text of Mesa's constitutional reform, nor any other text could change Article 230 of the existing Constitution since, in the original Constitution of the Republic of Bolivia, only a partial reform was possible. There was neither any legal way to introduce the concept and procedures for total reform. The Constitution that had been counterfeited clearly established:

"Part 4; Primacy and Reform of the Constitution.
Title 1; Primacy of the Constitution."

Article 228.
The Constitution of the State is the supreme law of the national legal order. The magistrates, judges, and authorities shall apply it with preference to the laws, and these with preference to any other resolutions."

Article 229.
The principles, guaranties, and rights recognized by this Constitution may not altered by laws that regulate their exercise, nor do they need previous regulation for their fulfillment.

Article 230.
This Constitution may be partially reformed, with a prior declaration made of the need to reform it, which will be precisely determined by an ordinary law approved by two thirds of members present in each one of the legislative Chambers.

1. *This law may be proposed at either of the Legislative Chambers, in the manner established by this Constitution.*

2. *The Declaratory Law for Reform shall be sent to the Executive for its promulgation, and may not be vetoed.*

3. *The Declaratory Law for Reform shall be sent to the Executive for its promulgation, and may not be vetoed. (Creo que esto es duplicado de lo anterior)*

Article 231.

1. *The first sessions of a new constitutional period of the Legislature shall consider the matter in the Chamber that formulated the reform and, if this [Reform] is approved by two thirds of the votes, it shall remand it to the other [chamber] for its review, which will also require a vote of two thirds.*

2. *The remaining processes shall be the same as the Constitution mandates for the interaction between the two chambers.*

Article 232.

1. *The chambers shall debate and vote on the reform, adjusting it to the provisions of the Declaratory Law for Reform that proposed it.*

2. *The sanctioned reform shall pass to the Executive Branch for its promulgation and the Republic's President may not amend it.*[42]

Article 233.
Anytime the amendment relates to the Constitutional Tenure of the President of the Republic, this shall be enforced only in the next period of government.

Supplanting means falsifying in writing, with words or clauses that alter the heretofore meaning contained, and this is exactly what has happened with the Constitution of Bolivia, in the Government of Carlos Mesa.

If the reader compares the constitutional text transcribed from the reformed constitution of 1994, he/she will note that NOWHERE WITHIN IT WAS THE TOTAL REFORM OF THE CONSTITUTION ALLOWED. It will be seen that NOWHERE IN ITS TEXT WAS THE TOTAL REFORM OF THE CONSTITUTION ALLOWED. That in the Constitution of the Republic of Bolivia THERE WAS NO POSSIBILITY OF TOTAL REFORM OF THE CONSTITUTION AND THE CONSTITUENT ASSEMBLY DID NOT EXIST.

On this illegal basis the Constituent Assembly takes off. Mustered by Evo Morales through a Law of 6 March of

---

42. Bolivia. Constitution of the State. Constitution of 1967 with reforms from 1994. 12 August 1994.

2006, it calls for the election of 255 constituent members to be elected on 2 July of 2006 and sets the 6th of August of 2006 as the date for its implementation.

3.2. The manipulation of the Constituent's Assembly

The Constituent's Assembly was convened on the 6th of August of 2006, under a premise contained in Article 3 of its Convening Law indicating that "it is independent and exercises the population's sovereignty, it does not depend from, nor is it subject to, the constitutional branches of government and that it has, as its only and sole objective, the total reform of the Constitution of the State". The seat for its sessions was set to be at Sucre, the constitutional Capital [city] of Bolivia.

Article 24 of the convening law established that "The Constituent Assembly shall have an uninterrupted and continuous period of sessions of neither less than six months, nor more than one calendar year commencing with the date of its convening." Article 25 of this same law established that "The Constituent Assembly shall approve the text of the new Constitution with *two thirds of the votes of the members present in the assembly,* in accordance with the provisions of Title II of Part IV of the existing Constitution of the State."

Article 26 of the Constituent Assembly's Convening Law also indicated that "Upon de conclusion of the Constituent

Assembly's mission, the Executive branch shall call a constituent *referendum,* at a date of no more than one hundred and
twenty days following the convocation. In said *referendum,*
the Bolivian population shall affirm through a vote of absolute majority, the project of the [reformed] new constitution
—in its totality—*proposed by the Constituent Assembly.*

A review of these guidelines upon which the Constituent Assembly based its organization and functioning, indicates to us its basic characteristics and determines its scope:

- The Constituent Assembly was supposed to be independent
  and not be subjected to any of the constituted branches
  of power.
- The seat, in other words, the place where it was supposed to
  hold its sessions was Sucre the Capital City of the Republic.
- Its tenure was to be six months, as a minimum and one calendar year, as a maximum.
- The approval of any new constitutional text was to be made
  by two thirds of the votes of the members present, which
  already was a trap on to itself, because the number of votes
  required by the [original] Constitution was *two thirds of the
  votes of the total membership.*[43]

---

43. Bolivia. Constitution of the State, 1994, Article 231.I. Mesa had
changed this provision by Law 2631 of 20 February of 2004 with its reform
resulting from the so-called October's Agenda.

- The project to draft a new constitution would be proposed
  by the Constituent Assembly and voted on it by an absolute
  majority of votes in a *referendum*.

If we dissect what happened, around this framework of
attributions such as; the setting of the nature of the Constituent Assembly, the place for it to be in session, the time
limits for its tenure, the number of votes needed, and the
need for the Constituent Assembly to be the one proposing
a new constitution, we shall see that all of the choreogra-
phy by Evo Morales from the Executive Power to have a new
constitution—at any cost—was a chain of illegalities and
malfeasance. Besides the superseding of the constitution to
incorporate its total reform into a totally new one and the
possibility to convene a constituent [assembly] –introduced
by Carlos Mesa, this supplantation demonstrates to us the
total invalidity of what ultimately turned out to be Evo Morales' Constitution.

What happened in reality was:

- That Evo Morales sought to control the Constituent Assembly from beginning to end, even to the point of mo-
  bilizing peasants', miners' violent groups and the so-called
  "social-movements" sustained by his government, to produce
  violent confrontations with casualties, as a mean to exert
  pressure on the Constituent Assembly's members and the
  citizenry.

- Having reached the one year tenure limitation of the Constituent Assembly, it had not approved anything drafted, and by the mandate of its own convening law that set the time limits to be in session, it was no longer empowered to continue. By law, after one year the Constituent Assembly simply was no more and its members had no legal standing to continue to meet, and most of all to approve any proposal. On the 3rd of July of 2007, however, this very Constituent Assembly that had not approved one single proposal for constitutional reform[44] decided to extend its own tenure to the 14th of December and sent to the National Congress this resolution. Congress approved, on the 3rd of August of 2007 the so-called Constituent Assembly Extension Law, extending its tenure be in session to 14 December of 2007 and establishing—among other changes—that those Articles which do not obtain the two thirds of votes of members present, shall be considered by the citizenry, thus setting up an additional mechanism through which to counter the required two thirds of votes in all decisions, and clearing the road to call yet one additional resolving *referendum* election. This way introducing yet one other element of malfeasance in the process.

- The political proceedings of the Constituent Assembly choreographed by Evo Morales produced violent clashes in the city of Sucre; these were initially attributed to matters dealing with pending issues regarding the seating of governmental

44. http://www.elcomercio.com/noticias/Asamblea-Constituyente-Bolivia-prorroga-diciembre_0_148785376.html

functions in the capital city of Sucre. On the 23rd of November of 2007, the leadership of the Constituent Assembly controlled by Morales violating its own Debate Regulations moved the place to hold its sessions into the military garrison "Liceo Militar Teniente Edmundo Andrade" in the area of La Glorieta, some 5 kilometers away from the city. This move produced the so-called "Massacre at La Kalancha" with the resulting death of several people and a number of others wounded as a result of violent clashes with governmental forces.[45] Facing a situation of rejection and social confrontation occurring in Sucre, Evo Morales through his MAS Political Party availed himself of a blockade by peasants who surrounded the Legislative Palace (Congress) and with the absence of congressmen from the opposition, steamrollered the night of 27 November of 2007 legislation empowering the leadership of the Constituent Assembly to call for sessions to be held anywhere in the country.[46] This way, the Assembly was moved to the city of Oruro where starting on the evening of Saturday 8 December of 2007 the governing party started the process to approve its own constitution "with the debate reduced to a minimum, with the hurried reading of the text and without reading any detail of each article . . . the surprising and violent change of the place for the plenary to meet at –that on Wednesday the 5th had been set

45. Merida, Isael. And You Want to Come Back? Evolution of a government. Press registers. 2009 Cochabamba, Bolivia, Pag. 310, 312, 313.

46. La Razón, Bolivia. La Paz, 28 November of 2007.

to take place at 'Lauca ñ', was part of the strategy devised by the MAS as a ruse to demobilize the opposition, revealed last night a MAS Party member of the Assembly" was reported by the press.[47]

• Bolivian news media now reported that "with two days to go for the deadline to deliver the [reformed] constitutional text, a group of 15 assemblymen from the governing political party, defines in substitution of the plenary, substantive, format, and style changes to the document approved in detail at Oruro."[48]

• Once drafted the new reformed constitution, the Constituent Assembly got to the 14th of December of 2007—their illicitly extended period—with a projected constitutional text.

• On 28 February of 2008, Evo Morales in an agreement behind closed doors with Jorge Quiroga Ramirez and Samuel Doria Medina, chiefs of the opposition's political parties with the greater number of seats in congress, promulgated Law 3837, adjusting it to its convenience—once again—the procedures for the Constituent [Assembly] and for his invented affirmation *referendum*.[49]

• Through Law 3941 of 21 October of 2008, Evo Morales secures the political agreement with Jorge Quiroga and Samuel

47. La Razón, Bolivia. La Paz, 09 December of 2007.

48. La Razón, Bolivia. La Paz, 13 December of 2007.

49. GALINDO, Eudoro. The Malignant Legacy, 2nd Edition, September of 2012, Cochabamba, Bolivia, Page 451.

Doria Medina to interpret Article 232 of the Constitution, determining that:

Article 1.

(Constitutional Framework). According to what is established in Article 233 of the Constitution, Article 232 of the Fundamental Law is hereafter interpreted.

Article 2.

(Interpretation). In application of the Republican Institutionalism, the principle of Popular Sovereignty, the Social and Democratic Rule of Law, determined in Articles 1, 2 and 4 of the nation's Constitution, establishing that it is the competence of the Honorable National Congress to contribute to the constituent project and to effect the necessary amendments to the text of the constitution approved by the Constituent Assembly, on the basis of the popular will and national interest, per special Congressional law, approved by two thirds of votes of its present members, the scope of constitutional Article 232 is interpreted as follows:

Article 232.

The total reform of the nation's Constitution is the sole and exclusive faculty of the Constituent Assembly, that shall be convened by a Special Convening Law that will indicate the forms and modalities of election of its members, it shall be approved by two thirds of votes of members present from the

Honorable National Congress and may not be vetoed by the President of the Republic.

Once the constituent process has been concluded and the constitutional proposal has been received to be considered by the sovereign population, the Honorable National Congress may make the necessary adjustments on the basis of the popular will and national interest, by special Congressional law approved by two thirds of its members present.

The adjustments may not affect the essence of the will of the constituent's members.

This way they also eliminated the Constitution's supremacy, which also implies that the Legislative Branch that is the representative of the people is limited by the Constitution and must subject its actions to what is prescribed in it.[50]

This is what had happened in and was caused by Congress, the modification and change of a text that was plagued by malfeasance (due to the loss of jurisdiction, the inexistence of the two thirds of the votes required, and the change of location), that the Constituent Assembly had approved. If the Constituent Assembly had acted without a legal standing, Congress did it usurping functions, because to be able to execute the political agreement between Evo Morales and Jorge Quiroga it self-empowered through Law 3941, with the lawful constituent faculties which belonged to the ordinary Legisla-

---

50. Lousteau, Guillermo. Democracy and Control of the Constitutionality, 2nd Edition, IID Editorial Fund, Miami 2009, Page 19.

tive Branch, that ended up in them being the main drafters of the text of the new Constitution. Afterwards it would be revealed that Quiroga and Morales had comprised a "secret commission" even keeping their own parliamentary caucuses in the dark, wherein they drafted the constitution, and wherein they had arrived at an agreement on matters such as the reelection of the President with the observance and guarantees of representatives from the Organization of American States (OAS).[51]

The Constitutional Referendum took place on Sunday the 25th of January of 2009, and ended up approving the text what is today the Constitution of the Plurinational State of Bolivia, "in an electoral process that ratified a marked division of the country Bolivians approved, with 58% of the votes, to back the project for the State's New Constitution, which the Government of President Evo Morales has identified as a cornerstone to provide continuity to his political objectives. The remaining 41.3% of the voters, who participated in the referendum, rejected the approval of the text."[52]

The National Electoral Court reported that the final vote count gave a 61.43% margin to the YES vote for the proposal for a new constitution, compared to a 38.57% of the NO votes.

---

51. OAS, Letter from Kevin Casas to Jorge Quiroga. SAP/OE-502/13.6 of June of 2013.

52. La Razón, Bolivia. La Paz, 26 January of 2009.

25 January 2009 Bolivia's Constitutional *Referendum*		
Yes or No	**Votes**	**Percentage**
Yes	2,064.417	61.43 %
No	1,296.175	38.57 %
Valid Votes	3,360.592	95.70 %
Annulled or Blank Votes	151.107	4.31 %
Total	3,511.699	100 %
Participation	90.4%	

The results broken down by departments, clearly evidenced a divided country. Of Bolivia's nine departments, the YES vote won in five and the NO vote won in four departments. The departments of La Paz, Oruro, Potosi, Cochabamba and Chuquisaca showed to be in favor of the YES to the proposal, on the other hand Santa Cruz, Tarija, Beni, and Pando voted for the NO. The difference in favor of the YES vote in Chuquisaca was a meager 1.54%.

The official graphic shows how the new constitution was approved by Bolivia's western departments and rejected by the eastern and southern ones from the country.

In spite of the close results and the division of the country that the results showed in a referendum seeking the approval of all Bolivians for a new constitution, the question of fraud and the electoral manipulation by the government to sway the process to its favor, is an additional variable that must be taken into account. On the day of the election, for instance, the president of the National Electoral Court, Jose Luis Exeni, rejected the possibility the indelible ink used to mark the right index of voters was of poor quality and easily erasable, but live tests conducted by UNITEL TV journalists showed the ink disappeared easily.[53] Complaints against fraud were not even registered and the government hastened to publish the final results to be able to promulgate its constitution.[54]

Constituent National *Referendum* of 25 January, 2009[55].				
Department	In Favor (YES)	Percentage	Against (NO)	Percentage
Chuquisaca	92,069	51.54%	86,555	48.46%
La Paz	885,513	78.12%	248,053	21.88%
Cochabamba	401,837	64.91%	217,269	35.09%
Oruro	128,911	73.68%	46,061	26.32%
Potosi	190,517	80.07%	47,420	19.93%
Tarija	63,754	43.34%	83,359	56.66%
Santa Cruz	256,578	34.57%	481,744	65.25%
Beni	34,233	32.67%	70,556	67.33%
Pando	10,403	40.96%	14,995	59.04%

The process that culminated with the drafting of a so called Constitution of the Plurinational State of Bolivia is a true iter-criminis, that is to say; it is an authentic path to a crime that is committed from the time it was thought of, and to the moment it was finished.

Up to the convening of the Constituent Assembly we have noted and described the conspiratory, preparatory, and propository acts. With the overthrow of the legitimate

53. www.adnradio.el January 25, 2009.

54. Bolivia, National Electoral Court (CNE), data, 15 February of 2009.

55. Bolivia, National Electoral Court (CNE), report of 4 February of 2009.

constitutional government in October of 2003, with the supplantation of the country's Constitution in 2004, the wrongfully called "reform" of Carlos D. Mesa who illegally introduced the idea of a total reform and the possibility of calling a Constituent Assembly and a referendum, with the actual convening of the Constituent Assembly, with the meetings of said Constituent Assembly and their handling, all the way to the approval referendum of the "new constitution", there were a number of illicit acts to consummate this criminal process.

The number, nature, persistence, and scope of constitutional and legal violations committed to get to the promulgation of Evo Morales' constitution can be described as an *iter-criminis*.

The crime committed is, without any doubt, the elimination of; the constitutional order, democracy, the Rule of Law, and the very existence of the Republic of Bolivia.

3.3. A Constitution for the Dictatorship

The day of the new constitution's promulgation, Bolivian media reflected on this event expressing that "in the midst of a polarized political environment created by the opposition from four departments (Santa Cruz, Beni, Pando, and Tarija) to the new constitution of the country (CPE), this will be promulgated today, in the city of El Alto, by president Evo Morales. The new statute obtained the support from 61.43% of the voters in the referendum of January 25, and it was estimated that its total application will lag 10 years.[56] "

Even those who were in favor of the new constitution's were critical, the analyst Paul Coca Suarez, for example, cited by the printed media, ascertained that it would have been ideal to have the new constitution approved with at least 70% of the votes in the constituents' referendum, which would have implied an important social backing of the constitutional text. According to Coca. the results were owed to the extreme polarization the country lived in and this was confirmed by the polls when four departments (La Paz, Cochabamba, Oruro, and Potosi) approved the new constitution project, but another four (Santa Cruz, Beni, Pando, and Tarija) reject it. The best example of this polarization was Chuquisaca, where until the last minute, it was not known who had won because the city voted NO while the countryside voted YES.[57]

"Do you swear to respect and have others respect the Country's New Constitution?" asked the President Evo Morales to thousands of people who had their left fist high in the air and their right hand over their heart—the symbol of the socialism they spouse—, "yes we do" they responded. On that historic day, he proclaimed promulgated; the new constitution of the country, the existence of the plurinational single state, and—on the side of economics—the communitarian

56. El Diario, La Paz, Bolivia, 7 February, 2009.

57. Bolivia, FM Bolivia, www.fmbolivia.com.bo 7 February of 2009

socialism", said Morales after signing the New Constitution. Peasants, native peoples, social movements, government officials, military, policemen, and dozens of journalists gathered in the city of El Alto, a developing metropolis on the outskirts of La Paz that is located at 4,000 meters above sea level, to witness an act that was dubbed as "historic."[58]

Aside from promoting and seeking a political advantage from the split in the Bolivian population, Morales and his government did not have any problem in publically stating the ideological nature of the Constitutional Charter now imposed upon Bolivia's citizenry (to the contrary, it was part of the political signal they meant to send). On that Saturday, starting with the promulgation of the new constitution, Bolivia was changed into a Plurinational State, in an event that Evo Morales considered "historic" and that he affirmed to be "the beginning of communitarian socialism".

"In this historic day, I proclaim the New Constitution of the State, of the Bolivian Plurinational State, of the beginning of communitarian socialism, starting with the new Constitution" Morales affirmed exuberantly in an heated speech that he gave at the city of El Alto, next to La Paz, the stronghold of the official governing party.[59]

There was the protocolar swearing with socialist symbology, Morales personally proclaimed the "communitarian

---

58. BBC Mundo.com http://news.bbc.co.uk/hi/spanish/latin_america/newsid_7877000/7877041.stm

59. Telam, 8 February of 2009.

socialism", ratifying the re-created constitution to his ideological alignment and promoted by Castro's dictatorship with Venezuelan monies. This way from the time of the proclamation by Evo Morales, this charter was presented as the instrument through which his government would exert total control over the country, which through time, would later be confirmed. What was being implemented was a constitution for the dictatorship.

The prologue of the new fundamental charter is an unequivocal and explicit evidence of its confrontational purpose and a declaration of an anti democratic political undertaking. Mixed with true historical passages worthy of vindicating, it has a confession of uprising actions, sedition, and conspiracy, like the "Water War" and the October's overthrow, that now are etched in the new constitution as the "War of October" when, in its second paragraph it states:

"The Bolivian people, of plural origin, from time in the depths of history, inspired by past battles, by the anti-colonial indigenous insurgence, by the independence, by the popular liberation battles, by the indigenous, social, and labor union marches, by the wars over the water and of October, by the battles for land and territory, and with the memory of our martyrs, we build a new State". This same introduction also announces the elimination of the Republic of Bolivia when it states: "We leave the colonial, republican, neo-liberal state in the past."[60]

Evo Morales proclaims in his constitution that he is ending the republic. The republic we understand to be the organization of the State whose maximum authority is elected, by the citizenry or by parliament, for a specifically determined period of time.[61] The new constitution imposed on Bolivians does away with the Republic of Bolivia and it ceases to be a "republican state".

Republic "in a comprehensive sense, is a political system founded upon the imperative of the Rule of Law and the equality of its citizens before the law as a way to stop the abuse by persons, the government, and the majorities who have greater power, in order to protect the fundamental rights and civil liberties of the citizenry, and from which we can never take away a "legitimate government."[62]

A legitimate government is only possible under the framework of a Republic, because this is the context through which the protection of the citizenry is guaranteed when being confronted by power, even the power of majorities, since even as a majority's rule, the fundamental rights of the people cannot be ignored.

---

60. Bolivia, New Constitution, Official Bulletin from the Plurinational State of Bolivia, La Paz, 7 February of 2009.

61. Royal Spanish Language Academy, 2001 Edition.

62. Wikipedia Enciclopedia.org.

To fully understand the severity and scope that Bolivia ceased to be a republic by the express declaration of authors of the New Constitution, much to the detriment of the rights of the Bolivian people, it is worth revising what the common elements that comprise the concept we call "republic" are:

- The incumbent's temporary tenure in a elected position. It is not possible to be indefinitely in a position, even when manipulating the reelection.
- The public nature of the government's actions. The secrecy of the state is not possible.
- The responsibility of politicians and government officials.
- The separation and control of power among the branches of government.
- The sovereignty of the law.
- The exercise of the rights of citizenry.
- The practice that spouses respect, and not intolerance, for opposing ideas. Guarantees for the right to dissent.
- Equality before the law.
- The competence as a prerequisite to be elected as a government official.

If we recall the process through which we get to the drafting of the new constitution with its inherent termination and deliberate disavowing of the republic to replace it with a Plurinational State, we can grasp the reason why the new constitution is grim for democracy.

The new constitution—which starts by eliminating the Republic of Bolivia—is structured in its political, economic, and social scope to disavow the basic elements that comprise democracy that, as we have cited, described, and remarked upon, in the earlier part of this text, are; *the respect for human rights and fundamental freedoms, having access to the power of Government with its discharge of obligations subjected to the Rule of Law; the conduct of periodic, free, and fair elections based on the universal and secret suffrage as an expression of the population's sovereignty; the system of plural political parties and organizations; and the separation and independence of the branches of government.*

From the very prologue of this constitution, it begins to discredit past periods of the country's history and to "take sides", it mentions the "grim" times of the colony, the indigenous anti-colonial uprising, the "wars over water and of October"; the martyrs of the constituent deeds, and it exalts and exacerbates the existing racism in the society. It declares the abandonment of the colonial, republican, and liberal State, to change Bolivia into a "Unitarian social State of plurinational communitarian rights". It is not necessary to be a constitutional law expert or a political scientist to realize that according to this prologue, Bolivia will no longer be a republic! Has the Republic of Bolivia ceased to be?[63]

The promulgated text has a racist content, is exclusionary and discriminating, and ignores human rights and the popula-

---

63. Gustavo Coronel. Opinioneideas.org, 9 January 2012. Written on 10 February 2009

tion's basic fundamental rights. Above it all, it seeks to end the Bolivian nation and divide Bolivians. "Bolivia's new constitution is a document of sad beauty, a kind of an anthropological curiosity in the midst of the XXI Century. It represents an unexplainable attempt to restore the rights and presence of the indigenous people in the life of a nation that had taken those away or had ignored them during years of turbulent history. In general, however, the drafters have swung the pendulum so forcefully that have taken this charter to the other extreme, to be almost racist, exclusionary, and discriminatory against certain sectors of the population who are different from the indigenous population. This document, with its undeniable good intentions, seems to consecrate the tribal, federative nature of a nation who, thus far, has been unable to find a solid collective identity."[64]

If we add to this that in the Population and Housing Census of 2013 almost 60% of Bolivians had rejected to be called indigenous, the gravity of the constitutional manipulation is even more noteworthy.

As the maximum leader of the illicit coca growers, Evo Morales dragged into the constitutional text the issue of the coca leaf considered by the United Nations organization[65] as a hallucinogenic and as the main raw material for the produc-

---

64. Gustavo Coronel, cited commentary.

65. United Nations Organization. Hallucinogenic Drugs' Convention, 1961.

tion of the crystal tropane alkaloid known as cocaine that is derived from it.[66]

Coca is now in Bolivia a "natural renewable resource" because Morales' constitution declares it "the native and ancestral coca (leaf) as the cultural patrimony, natural renewable resource from Bolivia's biodiversity; and a factor for social cohesion; in its natural state it is not a hallucinogenic" (textual verbiage, Art 384[67]).

The resulting destruction of democracy and institutionalism that Evo Morales has carried out in Bolivia using his constitution, was foretold the day of its promulgation, when the news media reflected through a peek of what had begun to happen, acknowledging that the new constitutional text gave more power to the indigenous population (who are a minority), reinforced the role of the Government in the economy, and recognized an autonomous state, at the departmental, municipal, and indigenous level that, in a political context, meant the presidential reelection that implied that Morales could— as he did—run again for the presidency when the general elections were conducted in December of that same year. Elections through which the new "Plurinational Assembly" would be elected to replace the existing National Congress.[68]

---

66. Wikipedia citing Aggrawal Anil, National Book Trust, India (1995), Pag. 52-3.

67. Constitution of the Plurinational State of Bolivia, Official Bulletin, Art. 384.

68. BBC World, 7 February of 2009.

The new constitution has within its text the carefully deliberate substitution of names and functions of governmental institutions. It substitutes; the Congress of the Republic for the Plurinational Legislative Assembly, the Supreme Court of Justice for the Supreme Tribunal of Justice, the Constitutional Tribunal for the Plurinational Constitutional Tribunal, the National Electorate Court for the Plurinational Electoral Organization with the Supreme Electoral Tribunal at its head, the Comptroller General of the Republic for the State's General Comptroller, the Public's Ombudsman Office for the Population's Advocacy Office, the Attorney General of the Republic for the State's Attorney General. This way, under the pretense that "the organization is no longer existent" or that "the function is no longer existent" Evo Morales and his government would conduct, in the months following, the figurative ransacking of those institutions and the firing of the constitutionally designated incumbent officials to replace them with people who are subservient to the regime who are subordinated to the authority and the whim of the president, now chieftain of all power, placed above the law and turned into a dictator.

If you compare the content of this imposed constitution to the constitutions of Hugo Chavez from Venezuela and Rafael Correa from Ecuador, we could have not expected anything different. The actual inspiration and drafting of these three constitutions of countries members of the ALBA or "Bolivarian" countries, was done by a group of attorneys from the University of Valencia; Viciano Pastor and Martinez Dalmau, amongst others, whose deeds and involvement were publicly recognized by the officialist constituents from Bolivia and the international news media.[69]

These self named neo-constitutionalist scholars teach a postgraduate course on constitutional law at the University of Havana, Cuba, proof of the hypocrisy that pretends to show that in a dictatorship Constitutional Law can be taught and disseminated. An attempt to show it as a new Latinamerican constitutionalist trend under the deceiving title of "new lat-in-american constitutionalism" that boasts "to have passed from the state of legality and the Rule of Law to a constitutional State of rights."[70]

As Viciano Pastor and Martinez Dalmau put it, the contributions of the new latinamerican constitutionalism consist of the radical application of the constitution's democratic theory through populist institutions: Indigenous derived constituent powers (excluding the constituents derived powers or constituted constituents, as the reforming powers are known), direct democracy mechanisms (referendum, plebiscite, popular revocation of mandates) and the election of constitutional courts.[71]

---

69. Washington Post, Tuesday 17 February 2009. "Latin-American document promotes revolutions; team of Spanish researchers helped to reformulate the constitutions of Venezuela, Bolivia, and Ecuador." by Joshua Partlow: Foreign Service from the Washington Post.

70. Interamerican Institute for Democracy, Paper Nr. 5, August of 2012, page 21.

71. Ob. Cit. Presentation by Guillermo Lousteau at the Congress of Latinamerican Studies Association (LASA), 2012.

With these arguments that attempt to formulate doctrine, the legal constitutional structure of the XXI century socialism dictatorships in latinamerica has been developed and organized.

The facts, as pointed out by former Ecuadorean president Osvaldo Hurtado, are that "the presidents of the so-called Bolivarian countries, once in power, schemed so that through a successive series of disguised mini coup-de-etats, were able to reject the constitutional legal framework under which they were elected and implemented a political system contrary to democratic principles. As done before by the military dictatorships, the constitution remained in force, but only in those areas that did not oppose the political objectives of the fledgling chieftain, until docile constituent assemblies would deliver the constitution that their acolytes had been ordered to write. The broad powers bestowed them allowed these to circumvent the law, yield unlimited power, and subject the legislative and judicial functions, subordinate the control organizations, restrict rights and freedoms, limit the pluralism, evade accountability, obstruct political alternation, and manipulate the electoral processes."[72]

_____

72. Hurtado, Osvaldo. Ob. Cit., Page 10.

CHAPTER 4

Consequences of Evo Morales' dictatorship in Bolivia

With his constitution as the fundamental legal basis, and in "compliance" of the new mandates established therein, Evo Morales launched the total replacement of the institutions throughout Bolivia, with his discourse to have founded a new State. But these actions were neither original to Bolivia, nor were they part of a talented plan by the Morales' government. It was something that had already been tried and was underway in Venezuela, Ecuador, and Nicaragua. The same one plan and the same charted transnational path that had careful oversight.

This process is clearly detailed by Osvaldo Hurtado when he says: "once the autocrats of the XXI century received the vast attributions the new constitution bestowed on them, through docile legislative organizations, the power of the presidential veto, or enabling powers, they constituted a maze of laws, whose tentacles maintain all democratic institutions trapped. Through the subjection of the legislative and judicial functions and control agencies, they comprised a system of political, economic, social, electoral, cultural, and communications' domination, they have relied upon to perpetuate themselves in the presidency and persecute, imprison, exile, silence, and intimidate critics and the opposition, so that no political alternative could emerge from therein. They have conformed communications' media conglomerates in order to control and manipulate public opinion, to restrict or eliminate freedom of speech, to harass, threaten, and on occasion expropriate newspapers, magazines, radios, and TV stations.

They also availed themselves of penal indictment proceedings, administrative actions, workforce inspections, tax audits, and other forms of intimidation through which they wanted to appear as though they were enforcing the law when in reality what they were doing was to persecute their adversaries in a malicious, discriminatory, and discretional way. Since the XXI century dictatorships control all governmental agencies, there is no justice, nor an independent judicial courts. The citizenry and society cannot defend themselves."[73]

Seeking the birthing of at least a continental concern over this grave situation, the former president of Ecuador accuses and demonstrates that "with each country's particularities, is what Hugo Chavez has been doing in Venezue-

---

73. Hurtado, Osvaldo. Ob. Cit. Page 11.

la since 1999, Evo Morales has been doing in Bolivia since 2006, Rafael Correa has been doing in Ecuador and Daniel Ortega has been doing in Nicaragua since 2007."[74]

This process has not escaped the international observation and analyses, although up to now there has only been silence, and disguised criticism from governments of democratic countries from the hemisphere and the world who due to political and commercial reasons have preferred, or currently prefer, to tolerate these governments already recognized as the dictatorships of the XXI century.

The government of Evo Morales in Bolivia, with these characteristics, has brought on very grave consequences for the country, to the point that after 30 years that military dictatorships delivered the government to democracy, Bolivia today has politically persecuted people due to an innumerable array of causes promoted by Morales himself and by officials from his government, it has political prisoners, and exiles.

The consequences of the lack of democracy in Bolivia are many and reach far beyond the criminalization of politics, or misuse of judicial powers to persecute the opposition that Evo Morales has instituted. Although the majority of Bolivians, thus far, do not have a clear grasp of the dictatorial nature of Evo Morales' regime and his project, the consequences of this way of governing make evident its nature

---

74. Hurtado, Osvaldo. Ob. Cit. Page 12.

and are clearly visible in areas such as; respect for human rights, political freedoms, freedom of the press and freedom of speech, the absence of the Rule of Law, in the electoral system and its procedures, in the quest for monopoly in political activities, in the subjection and misuse of the judicial, in the fight against narcotics trafficking, and practically throughout and everywhere national events take place, including those in the areas of religion, health, and education.

The dictatorial ways of Evo Morales' government does not, and will not, leave untouched or unaffected, any space of Bolivia's society, thus generating a heretofore unseen and extreme national crisis in its economic, political, social, and moral sectors.

This process towards the crisis has already begun and although it's currently disguised by apparent economic success and supposed social vindications, is taking the country and all Bolivians to a calamitous situation that will put the very existence of the nation.

4.1. Absolute control of power

Who has any doubts today that Evo Morales controls all power in Bolivia?

And "all power" means all four branches of government who Evo Morales himself introduced in his new constitution (the executive, legislative, judicial, and electoral powers). All government agencies whether these are for; control, tax revenue, supervision, economic activity, the armed forces and the police, the Departmental Governors' offices, and the municipalities proclaimed as autonomies within the constitutional context, culture, the press, public opinion, communications, investments, religious questions, agricultural production, the labor unions, education, health, sports, coca leaf, the disguised fight against narcotics trafficking. Everything.

But he, fundamentally, controls corruption, given that from the start of this total control concentrated in his person and his surroundings, corruption has surpassed all boundaries, to the point that the very dictator finds himself in the midst of a need to purge from time to time some of his collaborators who have gone too far and have made their corruption far too evident, and to whom protecting, now is very compromising.

All decisions are concentrated and must be brought to the knowledge of, and be authorized by "the chieftain"[75] either through his vice-president, or some other operator. The prosecutors, judges, mayors, commanders, entrepreneurs, labor union leaders, or any other citizen are part of the most diverse spectrum of Bolivians who have been forced to be subordinated, whether this is in order to obtain or keep a job, conduct large transactions, or simply in order to survive.

---

75. Adjective given to Evo Morales by Martin Sivak. Jefazo (Chieftain), An Intimate Portrait of Evo Morales.

The message from Evo Morales' government that has been etched in the minds of Bolivians is that "You can do well in Bolivia; you can have lots of success, and make lots of money, but don't mess neither with politics nor the government, and when the government asks you for something, you must be very generous". This same message is the same one attributed to a dictator of last century in our country: "to our friends, everything, to our enemies, nothing, to those indifferent with the constitution and the laws in effect." In every case, the rationality of totalitarianism is the same and the only things that have changed are the actors and the political rhetoric used to justify themselves.

4.2. Control of the electoral institution

Founded in the first transitory directives of the new constitution, Morales started dismantling the Republic of Bolivia and building a State with the objective to exercise total power over it.

Through law 4021 of 14 April of 2009, he convened elections regulating the procedures, conduct, surveillance, and control of the electoral process to vote on the Plurinational Legislative Assembly's constitution, the election of the President and Vice-president, and Departmental and Municipal Authorities, in the elections of 6 December of 2009 and of 4 April of 2010; besides the autonomy referendums, the elections of departmental assembly representatives and councilmen.[76] This law stated that in the institutional transition period, the National Electoral Court was responsible to manage the December 2009 and April of 2010 electoral processes, as well as the popular referendums that had been convened. This was due to the fact that the National Electoral Court had to be replaced by the "Electoral Supreme Tribunal" created by the new constitution.

The National Electoral Court presided by Jose Luis Exeni, an unconditional friend of Evo Morales, had been repeatedly accused of favoring the government, thus making the fundamental impartiality of this electoral agency disappear. Exeni resigned from his position, alleging personal motives, shortly after the December of 2009 elections had been convened, seven months prior to these elections. In his letter of resignation sent by Exeni to Morales he outlined an inventory of what he called "fundamental milestones" of the National Electoral Court, and the challenges the institution has ahead when dealing with the 6 December general elections. Among those so-called "milestones" he cited the inclusion of the special district boundaries demarcation, the acknowledgement of the need to allow Bolivian voters abroad to cast their ballot that enabled Evo Morales to organize and benefit from Bolivian voters abroad, especially those in Argentina.

---

76. Bolivia, Official Bulletin, Law 4021.

The opposition had asked Morales, on repeated occasions, to name a new person responsible for the National Electoral Court. Someone who is impartial and independent to guarantee clean elections. When Exeni resigned, Oscar Ortiz, a member of Jorge Quiroga's party and the president of the Senate, declared that Exeni's resignation ought to be "an opportunity" for Morales to name an impartial person who would guarantee "clean" elections. Ortiz declared that the President of Bolivia recover the tradition imposed through the fight for "impartial courts" that Sanchez de Lozada had led from 1989 to 1992 (although without mentioning it) to designate to the NEC a person of "known independence, capacity and effectiveness". Ortiz accused that one of the "greatest weaknesses" of Jorge Luis Exeni's management had been "his partialization with the officialism" and the "manipulation of the electoral rosters when the Government distributed, freely, of ID cards.

The former Vice-President of Bolivia, Victor Hugo Cardenas, a person of extraordinary credibility and respect in the country, declared at that time that "the resignation of Mr. Exeni is a democratic victory for the Bolivian people, because he was a sort of Minister of Electoral Matters for the President, there was no independence. It is the opportunity for the Government to return the credibility to the NEC."[77]

---

77. El Día (newspaper), Santa Cruz, Bolivia, 2 May 2013.

Morales designated Roxana Ibernegaray keeping the control of the electoral power, which continued to serve him in the "transition electoral process" that had been convened. In the elections of 6 December of 2009, Morales was reelected with 63.91% of the votes.[78] This election enabled him to control the "Plurinational Legislative Assembly", controlling two-thirds of the Lower House of Representatives, as well as the upper Senators' Chamber. In the lower House, of 130 Representatives there, Morales has 88 from his party and in the Senate of the 36 Senators, he has 26. With this predictable tools on hand, he proceeded to the implementation of his "Electoral Supreme Tribunal" comprised by seven members of which "at least two shall be of indigenous peasant native origin" and of all dependent agencies of this tribunal.

The political mechanism for the control of the electoral agencies by Evo Morales was now in-place, since the new constitution had provided that "The Plurinational Legislative Assembly shall elect six of the members of the Plurinational Electoral Agency, by the votes of two thirds of the members present. The President of the country will designate one of its members" and that "The Legislative Assemblies or Departmental Councils shall select by two thirds of the votes from the members present, a list of three

---

78. National Electoral Court from the Plurinational State of Bolivia. Minutes of the vote tabulation from national general elections and referendums of 2009.

candidates for each of the Court Magistrates of the Electoral Departmental Tribunals. From these lists, the House of Representatives shall elect by two thirds of the votes from members present, the members of the Electoral Departmental Tribunals, ensuring that at least one of its members belong to the indigenous, peasant, native peoples and indigenous, peasant people from the Department."[79]

4.3. The electoral fraud

Fraud is all actions contrary to the truth and righteousness to undermine the person against whom it is committed; it is any act which tends to evade a legal mandate, to the detriment of the State or of third parties.[80] Electoral fraud is any action or deliberate omission of intervention in an electoral process for the purpose to impede, alter, annul, or modify the results for the one's own benefit or that of a candidate.

Fraud is the permanent threat to every electoral process, especially for the fear that who is in a powerful political position may use fraud. In Bolivia after the general elections of 1989, tainted by electoral fraud during the tabulation of results to prevent the winning candidate to consolidate his majority in the senate. The MNR's candidate, winner of

---

79. Constitution of the Plurinational State of Bolivia, Art. Nrs. 206-II-III-V.

80. Royal Academy of the Spanish Language, 2001 Edition.

said elections, who was kept from getting to the presidency, conducted a political campaign called "Impartial Courts" aimed to depoliticize the designations of the members of the National Electoral Court and of Departmental Courts that up to then were earmarked to be occupied by the militants of those political parties with the greater number of votes in the elections. The impartial courts were a reality and this way, as an important advancement of democracy, it was accomplished that competent and skills officials, vested with impartiality, make up the electoral agencies since the elections of 1993. That situation of impartiality began deteriorating with the ascent of Evo Morales to power.

After the approval of the Constitution of the Plurinational State of Bolivia, and with the control of over two thirds of the votes in the Legislative Branch, Evo Morales seized every aspect of the Electoral Tribunal. This approach is common among those countries practicing the XXI Century socialism, because Chavez and Maduro in Venezuela, and Correa in Ecuador, and Ortega in Nicaragua, have all done the same thing. For the consolidation of total power, for the establishment of the dictatorships they have implanted, under the disguise of democracy, elections are indispensable and to win those elections they have to resort to electoral fraud.

Electoral fraud in Bolivia has been institutionalized by Evo Morales' government and is articulated before, during, and after the day of voting at the polls. The handling of public registries, the control of personal identification taken away from the National Police and delivered to a official party mechanism advised by "Cuban Advisors" makes the handling of the voters to conform to the whims and objectives of political powers in being from the Morales government. The circumscription boundaries, the registry and either the increase or decrease of voters in places where there are more or less government sympathizers, is another mechanism for fraud, placed into practice and made evident on 2013 with the manipulation of the National Census.

In the electoral campaign, the candidate from the officialist party Evo Morales has kept all competing political parties from campaign financing funds given by the State, based on the number of votes obtained in previous elections. This way, it is only him that can avail himself to unlimited resources from the State, from the coca leaf growers' unions, and from the unlimited political financing from Venezuela. The financing for candidates of opposing political parties has become almost impossible to obtain, because the government—furthermore—selectively suppresses all businessmen, or sympathizers who help opposition political parties, through administrative procedures and processes.

The universal free and secret ballot in Bolivia has been substituted in many instances by the so called "communitarian vote" that is nothing else than the collective induction towards a uniform vote in a given community due to the pressure exerted there by Evo Morales' government and with the promise of perks and stipends or the threat of sanctions through the suppression of investments for basic public utilities. This type of electoral fraud had already been applied by the peasants from Achacachi and the coca leaf growers' union from Chapare in the recall elections of 10 August of 2008 and the diriment and constituent referendums of 25 January, according to reports published by the observer missions from the Organization of American States (OAS) and the European Union (EU). The coca leaf growers union from Chapare and the peasants from Achacachi, the cooperative miners and peasants from Northern Potosi, sympathizers of the Movement Towards Socialism Party (MAS), announced they will apply the "communitarian vote" in the general elections of 6 December of 2009, to prevent any type of backing to the opposing candidates.[81]

Another means of institutionalized electoral fraud by Evo Morales is the prohibition that non-officialist candidates visit certain communities, thus preventing them to conduct electoral campaigns there, and even getting to the point of physically assaulting the opposition's candidates and placing their lives in jeopardy, as what happened to the indigenous leader Marcial Fabricano, whipped by coca grower union Morales' party members in May of 2009.[82]

---

81. Los Tiempos / La Prensa Newspapers, Bolivia, 20 July of 2009.

82. Hoybolivia.com. Official Party "Masistas" whip an indigenous leader Marcial Fabricano, 11 May of 2009.

Registry and Voting computerized systems introduced and disseminated from Venezuela are one other element of electoral fraud.

The favoring with prior decisions and legal interpretations, such as making Evo Morales eligible to run in a third election in 2014, through his Constitutional Tribunal, which was prohibited even under his own constitution, is evidence of the fraud prior to the elections that has already began to take place.

In April of 2013, the Plurinational Constitutional Tribunal (TCP) delivered a judgment that enabled president Evo Morales and Vice-president Alvaro Garcia to run in the elections of December of 2014. The argument is that since a new constitution is now in effect, a new State was formed and that, as a consequence, both only governed during only one period of government.[83] The scandal that ensued did not stop the fraud, since in this case the magistrate Gualberto Cusi, a member of the Plurinational Constitutional Tribunal (TPC) declared on 23 September of 2013 that the election of president Evo Morales in the elections of 2014 would be unconstitutional due to the Legislative Assembly usurping the functions of the Constitutional agency by drafting and approving the Law for the Application of Policy Guidelines. Cusi questioned that his colleagues had approved in April the recandidacy to Reelection of president Evo Morales and Vice-president Alvaro Garcia, to run in the

---

83. La Razon, Bolivia, 29 April of 2013.

next general elections for president, alleging that it would be a third reelection that goes against the Constitution of the State (CPE). He reminded everyone that when this issue was debated, he was on sick leave due to his health.[84]

There was fraud the day of the elections, such as what had been denounced during the constitutional referendum, by the easy was to wash off the alleged indelible ink that was supposed to keep any citizen from voting more than once. The fraud during this election also occurred through the "accidental" removal or change of the voting precints were citizens were supposed to have gone, especially in precints that were known to be contrary to the government. Bottom line, large quantities of citizens did not exercise their vote at the polls, even though they were issued certificates stating they voted, this was done "not to inconvenience" them.

Everything that could be used is used to favor, through electoral fraud, the candidates from the officialist political party who with such a guarantee, have already demanded his electoral apparatus that in the elections of 2014 they must garner 74% of the votes that is 10% more than those obtained in the elections of 2009. "The objective for me is to win with 74% of the votes, in each election we must increase by 10%, and it is in our hands" Morales said, when he inaugurated his political party (Movement Towards Socialism - MAS) in Cochabamba.[85]

---

84. El Diario, La Paz, Bolivia, 24 September of 2013.

85. El Deber, Bolivia, 6 October of 2013.

The electoral fraud in Bolivia is so inherent to the power of the dictator Morales that he doesn't even bother to abide by the electoral guidelines. What interests him is that having benefitted from the electoral fraud he has institutionalized, he continue to be presenting himself as a democratic president because he "wins the elections".

4.3. Control of the legislative branch

Having his constitution approved and his control over the electoral agency ratified, Morales put in motion the electoral process to be reelected within the framework of a new charter and for that reason he replaced the Congress of the Republic of Bolivia with the Plurinational Legislative Assembly, in which—as we already know—he has over two thirds of the votes from both houses, since the elections of 2009.

It is baffling, the accuracy with which Morales achieved such a supermajority, given that having 88 of the 130 members of the Lower House of Representatives, and 26 out of the 36 members from the Senate is enough to—in fact—do as you please. And that is exactly what he does, simulating democracy and having a "parliamentary opposition" that he keeps divided, intimidated, cooperating or criticizing within a framework of "an acceptable level of respect to the president".

For an adequate control and subjection of the "members of the assembly", senators and representatives, his own and those from the opposition, the new constitutional order of Evo Morales has left them uncovered by parliamentary immunity, establishing that members of the assembly will not have immunity. During his mandated term, in criminal proceedings, they will not be detained, unless they are caught "infragranti."[86] This constitutional verbiage, besides removing the immunity, makes express reference to proceedings under the criminal code, which demonstrates the reach of the threats under which the legislators must perform, who this way are precluded to even dissent.

Thus configured, the legislative agency with the Plurinational Legislative Assembly, it is seen that it becomes one very efficient instrument through which to legitimize the government's acts, and from which they cannot disguise their dependency.

To avoid the legislative agency from producing political leaders, as is usually the case throughout the world's democracies, the fundamental law of the Plurinational State of Bolivia, has established that "The mandated time of service for members of the Assembly is five years, after which they can be reelected for only one consecutive time."[87] It is clear that the dictator does not want new leaders to emerge,

---

86. Bolivia's Plurinational Constitution of the State (CPEPB), Art. 152.

87. CPEPB, Article 156.

reason why it is important to disarticulate periodically the composition of the legislative, avoiding the permanence of a legislator for more than two consecutive periods.

The new constitution has turned the members of the Assembly as salaried workers who could lose their employment for being absent from work for six consecutive days or a total of eleven days within a year, when establishes that "the assembly members' mandate is lost due to death, resignation, revocation of the mandate, executed penal indictment in criminal cases, or the unjustified abandonment of functions for a period greater than 6 consecutive days or a total of eleven days within a year, qualified according to regulations."[88]

The way things are in the Plurinational Legislative Assembly, one cannot say to be an independent agency, and worse yet, in the conditions under which it has been established, no one could exert effective legislative and fiscal controls, besides those dictated by the whim of Evo Morales.

4.4. Control of the judicial branch

The judicial system is responsible to put into effect the guarantees and rights of all citizens when confronting power and to settle, according to the law of conflict settlement any disputes which may occur amongst citizens. The judicial pow-

---

88. CPEPB, Article 157.

er's independence is one of the fundamental pillars of the Rule of Law. The judicial power is not only important for the correct functioning of democracy, but it is essential for social peace, political stability, economic growth, and sustainable development."[89]

The judicial power must only be subjected to the Constitution and the law, which means that from a separation of powers' perspective and in what corresponds to the judicial power, we have to ensure that Judicial Power is not subjected to none of the other powers of Government, whether this is the Legislative Assembly or the Executive. The magistrates not being subjected to imperative directives, different from or contrary to the law, without regard where these directives come from, are fundamental principles of judicial independence.

Throughout his government, Evo Morales has gained control for the political use of the judicial system, according to his interests. He began by destroying the justice system of the Republic, accusing judges, forcing them to resign, pursuing criminal prosecutions against them, and finally getting to change the name of the Nation's Supreme Court of Justice for the Supreme Tribunal of Justice, all only for the purpose of declaring vacancies and declaring terminated to all judges and magistrates that were constitutionally serving in all courtrooms.

---

89. Interamerican Bar Association. Judicial Power's Indicators of Independence.

All constitutional texts ensure the judicial power's independence. The Plurinational Constitution of the State declares that "the empowerment to impart justice emanates from the Bolivian people and is sustained on the principles of independence, impartiality, legal security, publicity, integrity, celerity, free of cost, legal pluralism, interculturalism, equity, service to the society, citizenry participation, social harmony, and respect for rights."[90]

But then, these principles are ignored when they establish the election for the magistrates of the Supreme Tribunal of Justice, through universal suffrage, determining that "The Plurinational Legislative Assembly will effect by two thirds of the members present the pre-selection of those candidates and the candidates from each department and shall submit to the Electoral Agency a roster of those prequalified applicants, for this agency to organize the exclusive one and only electoral process." Adding that "the candidates or any other person will not be able to conduct an electoral campaign in favor of their candidacy, under penalties of disqualification."[91]

The same selection and voting procedures were established for the members of; the Plurinational Constitutional Tribunal, the Magistrates Council, the Agro-environmental Tribunal. Please note, once again, the change in the names of

---

90. CPEB, Art. 178,

91. CPEPB. Art. 182 I.II. III.

the tribunals to fire the incumbents with the approval of the Plurinational State's Constitution, under the pretext that such agencies no longer exist. The Supreme Court of Justice was replaced by the Supreme Tribunal of Justice, The Judicial Council for the Magistrates Council, the Constitutional Tribunal for the Plurinational Constitutional Tribunal and the Agrarian Tribunal for the Agro-environmental Tribunal. Following this, judges were left without courtrooms, without instructions, and as a consequence were ceased from their functions so that Morales could proceed with the deceptive mechanisms for the election.

Establishing the election of magistrates through the universal suffrage and considering that with such a procedure there is no independence, impartiality, nor the possibility to have legal security. What really happened so demonstrated it, that Evo Morales having control of over two thirds of both lower and upper houses of the Plurinational Legislative Assembly comprised the list of magistrate candidates to his convenience, according to his directions, and then imposed the voting without any campaign.

The 16th of October of 2011, the voting to elect 56 magistrates to the highest judicial tribunals was conducted and the final results of this so-called judicial elections, showed that at a national level the votes casted in blank were greater in the election for the Agro-environmental Tribunal, the Constitutional Tribunal and the Magistrates Council, but not in the election for the Supreme Tribunal of Justice. Compared to the other judicial agencies, the election of the magistrates for the Supreme Tribunal of Justice was conducted by congressional departmental districts (circumscriptions), where it was evident that in four out of the nine departments of the country, namely; Santa Cruz, Beni, Pando, and Tarija, the votes in blank exceeded the other votes casted. Absenteeism was at 20.3%.[92]

With tribunals constituted this way, the control of the judicial by the executive was bolstered and the result that the country and international community can now see is that in Bolivia, repression has been judicialized and that politics and the government's repression are accomplished by means of the judicial system. Evo Morales himself accuses, or sends his proxy prosecutors or government officials to accuse, and the judges dictate steps, resolutions, or sentences according to what had been determined by the dictator.

4.4.1 *Some cases of judicial persecution*

Examples of this frightening situation are those cases of political persecution using the Justice System in Bolivia that with an enunciatively and not limiting character, are mentioned as follows:

---

92. Bolivia. Supreme Electoral Tribunal. Results from Judicial Elections of 2011.

- The so-called Responsibilities Trial against former President San-chez de Lozada, his cabinet of ministers and the Armed Forc-es' high command, to persecute them with repeated requests for the extradition of the president and his ministers and to currently have as his prisoners Generals Roberto Claros Flores, Gonzalo Rocabado Mercado, Juan Veliz Herrera, Jose Osvaldo Quiroga Mendoza, and Luis Alberto Aranda Granados;
- The massacre at El Porvenir in Pando to annul the Governor of that Department, Leopoldo Fernandez and to have him today as a political prisoner in the Departament of La Paz.

The so-called Case of Terrorism opened in Santa Cruz after the slaughter ordered by Morales in the Las Americas Hotel, to persecute, imprison, and extort all the civic, business, and youth organizations' leadership of Santa Cruz, forcing into exile personalities such as; Branco Maricovic, and others, and with dozens of regional leaders imprisoned.

- The persecution prosecution against Judge Tapia Pachi for his handing down an impartial resolution in the alleged Case of Terrorism, which forced him into exile.
- The prosecution and destitution of the Comptroller General of the Republic, Osvaldo Gutierrez, today in exile, in order to designate in his place a member of the officialist political party.
- The persecution proceedings against businessman Humberto Roca and his family with the bankruptcy of AeroSur and his extortion even abroad.[93]

---

93. The New Herald, Arrested for extorting in Miami the Anticorruption Chief of Bolivia. Jay Weaver, 6 September of 2013.

- The case of the Protected Indigenous Territory Isiboro Secure Park (TIPNIS) in order to build the so-called cocaine highway.[94]

- The more than 70 prosecution cases opened against the former president of the National Highway Services Jose Maria Bakovic.[95]

- The detention and persecution of the former President of the Central Bank, Juan Antonio Morales, still a political prisoner in La Paz and who was duly recognized internationally for his honesty and competence.

- The judicial persecution against the Governor of Cochabamba and presidential candidate Manfred Reyes Villa today exiled in the United States.

- The cases opened against the Governor of Tarija Mario Cosio, accused of corruption, and today exiled in Paraguay.

- The processes against the Governor of Beni, Ernesto Suarez Sattori, today with provisional freedom, and disqualified to be a candidate.

- The prosecution of the ex-prefect (governor) Sabina Cuellar and of her son, for alleged falsifying documents that included the search of her home.

- The judicial destitution of the Mayor from Sucre, Jaime Barrón, accused of instigating racist actions.

---

94. Veja Magazine, Brazil.

95. Deceased as a politically persecuted figure when this book was being edited. See Annex 8.

- The prosecution and destitution of the Mayor from Potosi, Rene Joaquino, accused by the government of economic harm to the state.

- The judicial persecution against Minister of the Supreme Court of Justice Rosario Canedo.

- The persecution trials against former Minister and Senator Guillermo Fortun who died as a jailed political prisoner in La Paz.

- The accusations against General Alvin Anaya, today under house arrest in Cochabamba.

- The trial of the former Governor of La Paz, Jose Luis Paredes, today in exile in Spain, who Evo Morales accused of being a "criminal".

- The accusation and detention of Civic Leader Felipe Moza from Villamontes, Department of Tarija.

- The jailing and persecution of Jacob Ostreicher, a business-man and US citizen, extorted and detained by the government who declared "I am a hostage of a controlled justice" and whose case has been presented to the United States Congress by actor Sean Penn, an old friend and apologist of dictators; Castro, Chavez, and Morales.[96]

- Accusation and judicial persecution against officials from the Jindal company (from India) for the mineral exploitation of iron from Mutun, including all executives and the attorney who have fled the country. The criminal accusations

---

96. El Deber, Santa Cruz, 11 November of 2012, Guider Arancibia.

would have as an objective to hide the acts of corruption and non-compliance by the Morales' government.

• The responsibilities trial opened against former President Eduardo Rodriguez Veltze for the so-called Chinese missiles case, to later negotiate with the public shaming for Rodriguez Veltze in exchange for this former President to serve as Evo Morales' ambassador on an on-going maritime dispute.

• The prosecution against the Ministers and High Military Command of former President Rodriguez Veltze for the same Chinese missiles, seeking to neutralize former General, and current Senator, Marcelo Antezana, following the liberation of the principal accused and Commander In Chief of the Armed Forces in that administration who is former president Rodriguez Veltze.

• Accusations and prosecution against opposing assembly members, subpoenaing them for depositions and criminal prosecution like that against Norma Pierola, Adrian Oliva, Yesica Echeverria, Alex Orozco, Luis Felipe Dorado, and others.

• Prosecution and intervention against the dean of the national press, "El Diario" to neutralize its line of defense of basic fundamental rights, today intervened by the government.

• The accusation and detention of journalist Jorge Melgar Quette in Riberalta, Department of Beni, for having taped and published a video in which Evo Morales' Minister Ramon Quintana promises the death of the Governor from Pando.

- The trial of Senator Roger Pinto to prevent him to continue his investigation of narcotics trafficking and the government. He took refuge and was inside the Brazilian embassy in La Paz for over a year, and now he is in exile in Brazil.
- The accusation and prosecution of the attorneys of many of the above cases in order to leave the accused defenseless.

4.4.2 Characteristics of persecution procedures

In the cited cases at the paragraph above, and in so many others that exist in Bolivia, some of the features of the criminal mechanism that the government uses are:

- The public and direct accusation by Evo Morales or by his closest collaborators in his behalf, for impressionable and disqualifying crimes that are basically centered in genocide, murder, terrorism, corruption, and attempts against the State.
- The accusations are always covering up the crimes committed by the complainant (plaintiff), or by Evo Morales himself and members of his inner circle; it has the political intent to neutralize or disqualify the accused, and to advance the institutional elimination.
- The accusation unleashes an intense propaganda and communications' campaign aimed at discrediting and eliminating the public image of the accused, in such a way that even be-

fore the prosecution begins, public opinion already considers the incumbent guilty, putting into practice the Stalinist and Castrist technique of "murdering the reputation."[97]

• The prosecutors proceed with a wide coverage by the official press, in such a way as for the accused to have little to no chance of being listened to in the public opinion debate that precedes and goes along with the prosecution.

• Arbitrarily they shift the territorial legal jurisdiction to take the case to courts of judges who are better controlled, generally in the city seat of government, La Paz and to be able to send detained victims to the high security jail at Chonchocorro.

• The judges, obedient to the regime, immediately impose enjoinment measures, generally the detention of the accused, the freezing of his assets and even those of their relatives, for the purpose of restricting the availability of any resource to enable their legal defense.

• Falsify the prosecution's data and supplant the mechanisms of proof, getting to extreme points, such as those related to the so-called Responsibilities' Trial for the events of October 2003, in which the authors of the criminal acts are now the accusers and witnesses.

• They protract and extend the prosecution proceedings to keep the accused under the enjoinment measures. The judges obedient to the regime then hand down sentences subjecting

---

97. Annex A "Murdering of Reputation by the Socialism of the XXI Century"

as political prisoners their victims who have no possibility of defense.

- In the course of the prosecution, government officials, prosecutors, and judges use their positions to extort huge amounts of bribes to citizens whom they threaten to include in their investigations; extorting also the accused in order to minimize the charges or exclude them from the trial.

- They apply, retroactively, laws and legal guidelines expressly dictated for the persecution and to effect accusations.[98]

- Conduct threats and start prosecutions against defense attorneys who are taken to trial and are intimidated in order to leave their clients totally defenseless.

- They extend the prosecutions and the accusations against family members, even underage citizens, in order to extort the accused who eventually leaves in exile.[99]

- Temporarily halt the prosecution, sometimes without detaining the accused, as a way to put pressure or intimidate them.

- They make public registry records disappear, destroy documentation, buy witnesses, and eliminate media digital archives that could be proof against the government accusations, such as the Google report which acknowledged

---

98. Law 004 of 31 March of 2010 denominated the Law of Marcelo Quiroga Santa Cruz.

99. The case of the youngest son and mother of businessman Humberto Roca has been denounced.

Morales' government's request to do away with some internet content.[100]

- Confiscate the accused and their relatives ID Cards, Passports, etc., thus preventing them to travel and depriving them of their constitutional rights of citizenship.

- Rewards with promotions and higher rank the prosecutors and judges that conduct themselves under the direction of the government and fully back them when there are complaints against them or when they are accused of criminal activity above the law.

- They setup a huge wall of officials, prosecutors, judges, and ministers so that the hand of Evo Morales is not visible, and if there are accusations of malfeasance, abuse, or irregularities, these protect him to the extreme that Evo Morales ends up accusing –but only through the media, the members of the judicial in order to wash his hands off guilt.

The simple samples mentioned above are, without any doubt, incomplete and not all inclusive, since not even a survey focused on identifying the legalized persecution by Evo Morales and his government would be able to encompass all of them. A book for each one of them would even not be enough and would run the risk of appearing to be fiction due to the situations of extreme abuse those accused are subjected to.

---

100. El Deber. Google reports that Bolivian government asked them to eliminate certain content from the internet. ANF, 19 June of 2012.

The victims, in many cases ill, imprisoned, exiled, or impoverished, do not wish their cases be noteworthy due to fear of greater reprisals against their friends and relatives, for fear that false accusations be made against them, or fear that new charges will be added to their prosecution, or fear that perhaps a government's "contact" will be tasked to keep a negotiation's channel open for possible negotiation that does not take place or that is used to extort greater sums of money.

Without doubt the cliché "fear is more effective than repression" said by Cayetano Llobet[101] when describing the control of Evo Morales and his government over citizens, through legalized accusations, portrays the whole picture of this level of dictatorial "effectiveness" implemented for Evo Morales by Castrist Cuba with Venezuelan monies in Bolivia.

People "with at least a bit of IQ"[102] understood that; the government must not be bothered with, they should not delve in politics, nor help the government's opposition in any way, they should be close to their government officials, they should give them permanent signs of support, or at least sympathy, to their undertakings. It is this logic and the significantly large financial earnings that explain how the

---

101. Diario de las Américas, Miami, 7 July of 2011. Cayetano Llobet. Themes Cycle, Interamerican Institute for Democracy.

102. Idiomatic expression used in some of Latinamerican countries when referring to someone not too intelligent or with a minimum level of prudence.

knees of a significant number of Bolivian bourgeoisie and entrepreneurs buckle and bow down to the coca leaf chieftain and his apparatus. It is still shameful nevertheless, but we cannot deny that it appears to be very reasonable.

What has been described is even worse than the concept of "defenseless", in other words; the abandonment, the lack of protection, and the situation of the party to whom the means of protection have been denied, or are negotiated[103] which happens when the judicial branch itself restricts or removes the means of defense for the accused.

They are false accusations that; hide the crimes of the accusers and/or have been forged to eliminate innocent citizens whose human rights –like due process, presumption of innocence, impartiality of the judges, and the non-retroactive character of the law, life, and even one's image are violated.

4.5. Corruption

An environment such as the one described above is fertile for the cultivation of an extended and uncontrollable corruption within its system of justice, given the premise that if judges are going to be subservient to the needs of the power in being and be corrupted in their handling of important

---

103. Cabanellas, Guillermo. Usual law dictionary, 12th Edition, Heliasta. Argentina.

cases, then they are free to apply their corruption throughout the rest of the cases. This situation has eliminated the slightest possibility of justice, giving-in instead to the presence of government connected networks that intervene as part of the corrupt system in any type of judicial cause.

Judicial corruption, however, is but one single consequence and part of the corruption that Evo Morales has submerged the country into, and that can be traced back to its origin vested in the coca-leaf chieftain, leader of the MAS political party, and President of the Plurinational State of Bolivia, himself.

Ever since his days as the leader of the coca leaf growers union, one of the features of his involvement has been that of disobedience of the law, the use of violence, and the practice of corruption. The organization of the Movement Toward Socialism (MAS) as a political instrument of, and for, the illegal coca leaf growers in the tropics of Cochabamba, was yet another act of corruption. Not being able to garner enough signatures needed to organize a Political Party according to the requirements of Electoral Law, they opted to purchase from a group of leaders who owned the acronym "MAS" that represented an off-shoot from the Falange Socialista Boliviana (FSB) political party.

Under the guise of humor, the book "Evadas"[104] has documented what are, without a doubt, expressions, dec-

---

104. Rodriguez Peña, Alfredo. Evadas, the book without an end. 3rd Edition, 2012.

larations, and confessions of violations of human rights'
and the Rule of Law, truly manifested acts of corruption by
Evo Morales:

- "With the constituent [assembly], with a slap in the face we
  are going to change the neo-liberal laws."[105]
- "To be subjected to the laws is to hinder ourselves, even if
  they say they are unconstitutional our decrees, our deeds,
  don't matter. . . I believe we should not have to wait for the
  laws, we must continue working with political decisions."[106]
- "The right pleaded in 2008 that there be no elections, that
  the President finish his five year mandate. There, I was totally
  disqualified. They attempted to cheat and we cheated them
  more interestingly yet."[107]
- "The Interamerican Press Association asks Evo to respect
  journalists, but I want to ask the Interamerican Press Association that as an institution they educate some journalists and
  teach them to respect me."[108]
- "Bolivia will support all States that fight against the United
  States' imperialism and, with the cooperation from revo-

---

105. Ob. Cit. Speech in San Julian, 20 June of 2006.

106. Ob. Cit. Speech in Entre Rios, 11 August of 2007.

107. Ob. Cit. Press Conference, La Paz, 28 September of 2010.

108. Ob. Cit. Declarations made in Potosi, 10 November of 2009.

lutionary nations; United States' imperialism will soon be destroyed."[109]

- "Politics are above the law. I want you to know that when any attorney tells me: Evo you are making a legal mistake, what you are doing is illegal, well I still do it, even if it is illegal. Afterwards, I tell the attorneys; if it is illegal, you make it legal. What have you studied for?"[110]

- "The accusation [of being] authoritarian, motivates me a lot."[111]

- "When I visit countryside towns, all women are left behind pregnant and on their bellies it says: Evo Delivers!"[112]

- "We are not just passing through the Governmental Palace, we are not visiting the Palace, we have arrived here for life… we have recovered what was ours and it will be for life!"[113]

These statements that were publicly disseminated and that if made under some other context could even be funny, are another important element to corroborate the true nature of the regime that governs Bolivia today, that of a dictatorship that manages the country according to its whims and forever.

---

109. Ob. Cit. During Evo Morales' visit to Iran. Tehran, 27 October of 2010.

110. Ob. Cit. Announcement of oil pipe gas duct works, 20 July of 2008.

111. Ob. Cit. Evo Morales' response to United States National Director of Intelligence James Clapper, who labeled him as an "authoritarian populist", Santa Cruz, 2 February of 2012.

112. Ob. Cit. Sacaba, 27 March of 2010

113. Ob. Cit. Speech at the VII Ordinary Convention of the MAS-IPSP Political Party, Oruro, 10 January of 2010.

There is proof abroad of Evo Morales and his government's corruption. Officials close to him and of his trust are those that are in federal jails by order of United States' justice. His Chief for the fight against narcotics trafficking was condemned to 14 years of prison for cocaine trafficking after he was detained in Panama by the DEA.[114] And, his chief for the fight against corruption was jailed without the benefit of bail, and awaits prosecution with a possible sentence of up to 25 years of time in jail, after his arrest by the FBI for extorting Bolivian businessman Humberto Roca Leigue, persecuted by Evo Morales and his government.[115]

4.6. National Security

The security of the nation has been replaced, during Evo Morales' time, for the security of the regime, for the security of the dictator and his project in the regional framework denominated Alba, or socialism of the XXI Century.

For this, even from before the successful coup-d-etat of 17 October of 2003, the coca leaf growers' union chieftain had access to the Castrist Cuban intelligence support that operated out of its embassy in La Paz. Once in power, the

---

114. El Comercio, Lima. Reuters News Agency. Former Evo Morales' anti-drug czar condemned in Miami to 14 years in jail, 23 September of 2011.

115. Miami Herald. Chief of Anti-corruption in Bolivia arrested for corruption in Miami, 6 September of 2013.

presence of Cuban intelligence and Venezuelan military has been overt and openly uninhibited, to the point that the presidential security detail, trainers, pilots and advisors have been from those two countries.

Evo Morales has conducted the systematic dismantling of the Armed Forces' institutionalism, starting with the military commanders. Since Bolivia returned to democracy in 1982, each government's administration had respected the seniority, hierarchy, and individual merit for the promotion of military and police commanders, having made the political decision of designating from amongst the top three officers or Generals from each force. This good practice is a thing of the past as it has been substituted by the president's political decision, which, in each case, is to favor or enable the continuation of his dismantling project.

The media, from the beginning of Morales' government, included in their coverage his attacks against the Armed Forces' institutionalism: "The honeymoon is over and we now have to go to work" Evo Morales told his ministers, but 24 hours later he caused his first scandal, by retiring into the inactive reserve 28 military accused of delivering Chinese missiles to the United States...Commander In Chief of the Armed Forces by constitutional empowerment, Morales designated Brigadier General Wilfredo Vargas as Commander In Chief of the institution and General Isaac Pimentel as Commanding General of the Police.

His designations were questioned as "incorrect and unjust" by army General Marco Antonio Vasquez who was next on line by direct succession to the Commander's position "if he had not been redlined."[116]

The Armed Forces have been taken out of their institutional context, the change of doctrine starting at the military academies has gotten underway. Commanders are forced to practice politics and subject themselves to the policies of the government, intervening with support opinions to the regime.

From the government and the subjection of military Commanders, the so-called "total reform of the Armed Forces" has gotten underway and will continue to the year of 2025. The politization led the Commander In Chief of the Armed Forces, Edwin De la Fuente, to declare on the institution's anniversary date, the 7th of August of 2013 that the Bolivian military institution has entered into a reforming process which, way ahead, will enable the Armed Forces to be doctrinally decolonialized and will convert into an anti-imperialist force. "The strategic vision of the reform seeks to constitute a doctrinally decolonialized, anti-imperialist Armed Force, with a high degree of operational effectiveness."[117] Pleased, Evo Morales celebrated the statements made by the top leader from the Armed Forces because "it

---

116. Caracol, 25 January of 2006.

117. El Diario newspaper, La Paz, 8 August of 2013.

reaffirmed their socialist and anti-imperialist vocation in defense of the homeland" and explained that the Armed Forces have a nationalistic character because, along with the social movements, "are the only ones" that can ensure that natural resources are not again privatized; socialist, because they work delivering bonuses and stipends, and also because they will be postured to contribute to national development with technologies; and anti-imperialist, because they are "on the people's side."

Thus, the Morales' dictatorship placed the Armed Forces at his service, indoctrinating it and forcing its commanders to declare them socialist and anti-imperialist. In any case, they are no longer the Nation's Armed Forces at the service of the homeland, a fundamental institution, defender and guarantor of the constitution. They are Armed Forces only at the service of a totalitarian regime.

The government has humiliated the Nation's Armed Forces and in so doing, has humiliated the Bolivian population by rendering multiple tributes, erecting monuments, and placing large photographs in government's offices—including the presidential office—of guerrilla fighter Ernesto Che Guevara killed in Bolivia as a result of his guerrilla armed incursion. While Evo Morales and his government pay tribute to the invaders, Bolivian military veterans, former fighters against the guerrillas, are outcast, forgotten and humiliated. The Morales' government never paid tribute to homeland's defenders killed or wounded by the foreign invaders, in the guerrilla war from whom Bolivia defended in this historic episode. In any case, this situation is not surprising since Morales has converted Bolivia into an updated version of the XXI century socialism, a country with Castrist ideology.

As if what has been described was not enough to show that the XXI Century Socialism project or "Alba" comprised by Cuba, Venezuela, Ecuador, Bolivia, and Nicaragua, is an absolutely dictatorial and anti-democratic project, Evo Morales has participated and allowed the creation of the "ALBA'S SECURITY AND DEFENSE SCHOOL" in Bolivia, an institution created by the decision of the XXI century dictators who met at the so-called "Alba's Summit in Cochabamba" on the 17th of October of 2009.

Castro, Chavez, Correa, Morales, and Ortega decided to create this school—under the façade of a defense academy—as a response to the foreign military influence and to develop one's own doctrine." They established as an objective "to strengthen the integration process of the ALBA countries through the *training of civilian and military personnel with an anti-colonialist, anti-imperialist, anti-capitalist focus.*" In a document signed in Santa Cruz (Bolivia) they adjusted the objectives by indicating they are: "to develop defense systems and integrated strategies in the face of common threats" and "to provide the development of the Armed Forces to have a real deterrent capability when facing external threats." They also enunciated that it will be "a

school for advanced military studies for officers from eight
countries; Cuba, Venezuela, Nicaragua, Ecuador, Honduras
(where the Zelaya project failed), Antigua and Barbuda,
Dominica, Saint Vincent, and the Grenadines."
Towards this end, they built facilities in the area of
Santa Rosita de Paquió in the town of Warnes, 14 miles
from the city of Santa Cruz, in an area considered geo-politically strategic because of its geographic location, as well
as the population control that can be exerted from there.
At the opening ceremony, on 31 May of 2011, of the facilities constructed the Minister of Defense from Iran,
Ahmad Vahidi (with an international capture order from
Interpol due to his participation in the terroristic attack
against the AMIA Jewish Association in Buenos Aires in
1994) was a guest in attendance. He was personally greeted
and entertained by Evo Morales (they were photographed
together at the official ceremony). This precipitated the
quick departure of the Iranian, without neither Morales
nor his government paying attention to the international
capture order. The unofficial explanation of the Iranian's
presence was that they had contributed some funding for
the construction, as if the deep pockets of Chavez then had
needed such assistance.

On 25 July of 2013, within the framework of a so-called
"1st International Security and Defense Seminar" presided
by Evo Morales in the city of Santa Cruz, the high military
commands from Bolivia, Nicaragua, Cuba, Ecuador, and

Venezuela, as members of ALBA, subscribed the "document to promote the school for the ideological-military professional development" with the "purpose to establish and make viable; the school's operational budget, establish an organizational wiring diagram, establish its human resource requirements for advisors, instructors, and students." Colonel Hernan Fuentes was named Commander of this school. Evo Morales expressed in his behalf and on behalf of the Presidents of ALBA countries that "we have the obligation to change the doctrine of our Armed Forces; we want Armed Forces which are ideologically, politically, professionally developed..."

All of this –even under the laws of ALBA dictatorships—are at the very least, crimes of "treason to the homeland" and "subjugation to a foreign power." Under the laws of these dictatorships it is a necessity in order to seize the legitimate use of the forces and to organize their own armed groups, deinstitutionalizing as a whole the Nation's Armed Forces.

With regard to the Bolivian Police, the level of politization there could not be greater and goes hand in hand with the rampant corruption and its institutional elimination. It will not be long when Evo Morales will replace it with a National Political Police and will subdivide its institutional functions, just as he already has done with the national identification, licenses system, and others.

4.7. Presence of foreign meddling

From the time of Evo Morales' arrived to power, the presence of Cuban and Venezuelan agents in different institutions has been evident and extensive. They started with areas such as security, military, police and intelligence, to the extreme—just as we have described it—that currently they control the personal identification services for all Bolivian citizens, with which they have the possibility to reidentify or falsely identify any foreign person, including members of criminal networks and terrorists that roam the world with documentation as if they were Bolivian citizens.

The presence of Cuban physicians, for whom Bolivia besides pays Cuba has proliferated, displacing Bolivian physicians who have conducted public protests and have been repressed by the government. The quality of health care provided by the Cuban physicians has been questioned due to their low professional qualifications. Bolivian autonomous universities have rejected to validate medical academic titles for those who graduated from Cuban universities and consider medical school curricula to be insufficient. Evo Morales has, personally, ordered that the State validate their studies.

In the area of education, Morales has delivered the task of rural literacy to the "Cuban cooperation" and has self-attributed to have ended illiteracy, when successive Bolivian governments have been dealing with this problem, practically from the time of the educational reform in the decade of the fifties, a byproduct of the National Revolution. Obviously the presence of Cuban educators is part of the indoctrination and change of Bolivian children and youth's mentality, a vital step for the totalitarian plan.

The intervention of Cuban-Venezuelan governments in the area of nationalized telecommunications, is less notorious but strategic because they have launched, from Bolivia and in coordination with the remainder of ALBA countries, a support network to their means of communications, control over Internet networks, and eavesdropping of the citizenry's and institution's communications that are deemed subject to investigation. While they do this from the government, they get a mouth full of solidarity complaints backing the North American eavesdropper.

The Cuban presence is practically an occupation of the territory and vital functions in Bolivia. Evo Morales has delivered the control over the postal system to Cuba, to the point that is not unusual to see postal stamps paying tribute to those who the Castrist dictatorship calls heroes and who are condemned spies in the United States, and others allusive to the so-called solidarity with Cuba.

The Venezuelan intervention is more evident in the military and economic areas, although in many cases under the disguise of being Venezuelan, Cuban personnel are really acting disguised with Venezuelan citizenship and military hierarchy.

Democratic states do have foreign cooperation, but the presence of the Cuban and Venezuelan governments in Bolivia is far too distant from what cooperation entails, because theirs is really the direction of the internal affairs of Bolivia, demonstrated by the fact these interventionists have very little to help with in areas in which Bolivia was far more advanced in, such as; the literacy campaign, the universal maternal-infant universal health insurance for example, education with the educational reform underway by national consensus, telecommunications, the postal system, and in reality in all the areas chosen by the interventionists to have control over and expand their ideological influence.

4.8. The fight against narcotics trafficking

It is difficult to imagine how the highest leader of the harvesters' union of illegal coca leaf, the main raw material for narcotics traffickers, could keep that condition, attempt to legalize the coca leaf, expand the cultivation of the illicit coca leaf, while at the same time "fight against narcotics trafficking."

Evo Morales, has solved this dilemma in a very simple way; on one hand, he promotes the expansion of the cultivation of the illicit coca leaf and the integration of the drug production circle to the point that in almost each coca leaf harvester's case, they are also producers of cocaine base paste; and on the other hand he decreases, unattends, eliminates, corrupts, the structure for the fight against narcotics trafficking and expels the most important and effective allies in this task.

The expulsion of the antinarcotics U.S. Drug Enforcement Agency (DEA) accomplished by Evo Morales' "personal decision", is not an isolated case, an insignificant case, or a simple act of the regime's anti-imperialistic ideology. When we consider the intelligence support, exchange of information, and control of the anti-narcotics forces in which, among other things, the DEA cooperated, we can easily conclude that the efficiency and transparency of the fight against narcotics in Bolivia has ended, thus meeting the political intent of the President of the Plurinational State.

On the 1st of November of 2008, the President of Bolivia, Evo Morales decided to "indefinitely" suspend the mentioned U.S. antinarcotics agency's operations, after lobbying accusations of "spying and conspiring" against his government. Morales accused the United States' DEA (Drug Enforcement Agency) of financially supporting the civic prefectural intent to overthrow his government and ordered the indefinite suspension of its activities in Bolivia. "It is a personal decision; starting today the activities (in Bolivia) of the North American DEA are suspended. We have the obligation to defend the Bolivian people's sovereignty" declared Morales, who that past August had revoked the flight authorization of aircraft from this antidrug agency.[118]

During the administration of Morales and following the increase of coca and cocaine production in Bolivia, the increase of corruption related to drug trafficking, the increase in the presence of the international mafia in the Plurinational State, and turning Brazil into its main trafficking market, important news media and international investigators began to ask first, and then sustain that Bolivia had turned into a Narco-State. Following are some data on this particular issue:

- According to "Univisión Investiga", Mexican narcotics trafficker Joaquin "El Chapo" Guzmán has taken advantage from the environment of corruption and complicity that Bolivia lives with, in order to expand his business' horizons and send one of his sons to this country. According to Bolivian government's intelligence documents obtained by Univisión Investiga. The picture of a Bolivian narco state that is described in those reports shows an intense level of activities of the Sinaloa, Norte del Valle de Colombia, and Primer Comando Capital de Brasil, drug cartels in this Andean country. "Chapo's son was enrolled in flight school for pilots in Santa Cruz and crashed into the city. That was

---

118. La Razon / EFE. Bolivia, 1 November of 2008.

last year, he was enrolled with a Bolivian name" stated one of the reports.[119]

• The same investigation reports: The complicity levels of Bolivian authorities with international drug cartels are known by the United States government, according to Douglas Farah an analyst expert in Bolivia who maintains contact with antinarcotics federal organizations. "United States' authorities know these documents, have seen the documents, and these come to reinforce what is coming out in the trial of General Sanabria" affirmed Farah, president of IBI Consultants and a former reporter for *The Washington Post*. "I believe that without this context I would not have necessarily taken as seriously the documents and date there."[120]

• Brazilian news journal magazine Veja reported that Jerjes Justiniano is the ambassador from the Bolivian narco state in Brasilia: Duda Teixeira. The foremost reason for the political persecution of senator Roger Pinto Molina who requested asylum in the Brazilian embassy in La Paz was a report that he delivered to the Presidential Palace (Palacio Quemado), seat of the Bolivian Executive, in March of 2011. The package had copies of reports written by intelligence agents from the Bolivian Police which revealed the participation of members from President Evo Morales' political party Move-

---

119. Univisión News. Gerardo Reyes, Intelligence Reports describe Bolivia as a Narco-State, 7 September of 2011.

120. Univisión News. Inf. Cit.

ment Toward Socialism (MAS), and of public officials at the highest echelons of the government in narcotics trafficking.[121]

• With the heading "Cocaine's Republic" Veja affirms "The President of Bolivia, Evo Morales takes pride in promoting coca plantations, the raw material for more than half of the cocaine and crack consumed in Brazil, under the argument that its leaf are useful to make tea and traditional medicines. However, according to estimates from the United Nations Organization (ONU) only one third of the coca harvested in this country is enough for such a demand. The remainder supplies narcotics traffickers, and contributes to corrupt the lives of almost one million Brazilians and their families. Recently, evidence has surfaced that the complicity of the Bolivian government with narcotics traffickers goes far beyond a simple defense of the interests of the coca leaf harvesters or the planters of coca."[122]

4.9. Worship/Cult of the dictator

The worship of the person and of the personality of the leader is, without any doubt, one of the features of the dictatorial regimes. According to the Soviet dictionary of philosophy the worshiping of a personality is the blind inclination to be under the authority of some figure, the excessively

121. EJU. Bolivia. 1 September of 2013.

122. Veja Brazil. 11 July of 2012, Page 1.

weighting of his real merits, the conversion of a historical personality is a fetish.

The theoretical basis of the worshipping of a personality rests in the idealistic conception of history, according to which the course of this personality is not determined by the acts of the population's masses, but by the desire and will of great men (chieftains, military heroes, noteworthy ideologists).

Differing from propaganda, whose objective is to disseminate the regime's ideology, the purpose of worshiping the personality is to reinforce the political position of the leader. The message behind the worshiping of the leader is *"In this regime, the only person that matters is me."*[123] In dictatorships it is often a way of worshiping the person of the dictator[124] and has turned out to be typical of dictatorships such as those from; Stalin, Hitler, Mussolini, Franco, Mao, and Fidel Castro as examples.

These concepts and historical examples help to better understand and ratify the dictatorial conduct of Evo Morales who, through a Supreme Decree 28807 issued on 21 July of 2006, a few months after he had assumed the presidency, declared "the town of Orinoca as a Historical National Patrimony and the house where his Excellency the

---

123. And Then There Was One!, The Politics of Authoritarian Rule, Page 79.

124. Wikipedia. http://es.wikipedia.org/wiki/Culto_a_la_personalidad.

President of the Republic Evo Morales Ayma was born in as a Historical Monument."[125]

This declaration is based in that Orinoca, being the capital of the county of the same name, located in the Municipality of Andamarca, Province of South Carangas from the Department of Oruro, and cradle of the President of the Republic, becomes indispensable to highlight this place as a fundamental part of the nation's history.

Moreover, he declares that towards this end, it is necessary to create an interactive museum on-site, which will enable everyone to know and reflect over the history of peasants' movements and original ancestral indigenous population of Bolivia and the creation of a Center of Excellence for Indigenous Studies, which will have coverage by the Ministry of Production and Micro enterprises.

The emission of postal stamps referring to the two inaugural ceremonies of President Evo Morales in 2006 as President of the Republic, and in 2010 as President of the Plurinational State, wearing different garments, besides the other series of postal stamps with his image, are acts of worshiping the personality that reoccur in the Morales administration.

Applying this worshiping concept of the dictator, Evo Morales has ordered the minting of several series of coins with his image. No other democratic president in Bolivia had done this. Numismatic Panorama, under the heading

---

125. Bolivia's Official Bulletin, D.S. 28807 from 21 July of 2006.

"Controversial coin with Evo Morales' face" reported: "At the request of Bolivia, the minting house of Chile has minted five special golden coins with the effigy of Evo Morales to commemorate the bicentennial of independence in America. The golden coin has prompted great indignation in the Andean country, both in the opposition as well as in several social sectors due to two concrete reasons: The first, that the minting was not done in Bolivia; and the second, that it is a self-tribute by the President himself and moreover that it was minted in gold." Representatives from Chile's Mint House delivered the coins to Evo Morales at the Presidential Palace, five samples of the coin, from a mint batch of 10,000 coins minted in Nordic gold."[126]

The Central Bank of Bolivia presented on 5 August of 2010 "a lot of 7,000 coins commemorative of the principles and values of the new Plurinational State's Constitution in which the image of President Evo Morales Ayma stands out." The coins are minted with a smooth high quality silver 933 border, weighing 27 grams, minted by the Royal Mint House of the Netherlands.[127]

In this same worship of the personality, Evo Morales with his control over the Departmental Legislative Assembly, enacted by Law 045, the designation of Oruro's airport with his name, producing a justified reaction from the pop-

---

126. Spanish Association of Numismatic Professionals, www.acnp.org

127. Los Tiempos newspaper. Cochabamba, 8 August of 2010.

ulation of Oruro in defense of the first Bolivian pilot Juan Mendoza, whose name bore such airport practically from its very beginning of operations.

A conflict was generated that took over 30 days of demonstrations that concluded with the repeal of the questioned law. This way, Juan Mendoza's name was returned to the Airport of Oruro that bore, for 43 days, the name of Evo Morales. "Law 045 is null and without any legal effect in its totality" says the first article of a consensually agreed law between the Directory of the Departmental Legislative Assembly, the Departmental Central Labor Union (COD), the Civic Committee, and the Only Federation Union of Peasant Workers from Oruro, among others.[128]

In every act of vainglory and worship to his person, Evo Morales has violated the law dated 7 October of 1941, that provides for any monument erected anywhere within the Republic's territory or outside of it, at the behest of the Government, or with governmental funds, to perpetuate the memory of some historical personality or event, shall be the subject of a Special Law, and that eligibility for this monument will only be reserved for deceased personalities, adding that it is absolutely prohibited to designate provinces, populations, colonies, schools, ports, roadways, bridges, railroad stations, plazas (main squares), avenues, streets and facilities, or public places of any kind that are dependant from the State or municipal-

128. La Razon newspaper, 23 March of 2013.

ities, with the names of persons alive without regard to how eminent the services rendered to the country or any locality may be.

4.10. Violation of human rights

All the points described up to here, demonstrate the violation of human rights and of fundamental rights by the government of Evo Morales. There are, however, cases considered as "banner" cases that reveal the total dictatorial nature of the regime.

The New Democracy Foundation[129] summarizes as grave violations of human rights the following cases that are not investigated:

• La Calancha. In November of 2007, the result of moving the Constituent Assembly to the Grand Mariscal de Ayacucho theater in the city of Sucre. There was a brutal repression leaving a balance of three dead.
• Urresti Case. In January of 2007, young university student Cristian Urresti was assassinated by coca-leaf harvester peasants' mobs that had taken over the 14 September main square plaza in the city of Cochabamba. No one has been charged.

129. New Democracy Foundation. Human Rights Observatory. Chronological report of Human Rights violations that occurred in Bolivia, 2013.

- Cárdenas Case. In April of 2008, peasant sympathizers of the MAS political party invaded the home of former vice-president Victor Hugo Cardenas at Senk'a Jawira, Omasuyos province of La Paz. The mob beat the former vice-president's wife and children.

- 24 May Case. In May of 2008, a group of students from Sucre forced peasant sympathizers of MAS to kneel and beg for forgiveness, reason why the government initiates suit against members from Interinstitutional Committee.

- Repression in Chaparina. The 25th of September, in San Lorenzo de Chaparina, next to Yucumo (Beni), 500 policemen storm and charge against marchers who were defending the TIPNIS (Ecological & Protected Indian Reserve) leaving hundreds of wounded.

- Repression of Disabled. On 23 February of 2012, a hundred policemen repressed a march by disabled persons when these were attempting to enter into the city's main square (plaza Murillo).

- Quispe Case. On 12 March of 2012 Juana Quispe, Councilwoman from the Ancoraimes municipality of La Paz, was brutally assassinated. Removed from her position in an unfair and illegal manner, returned to fulfill her mandate and after 32 days of her return, was assassinated.

- Mendizábal Case. On 29 May of 2012, Judge Ximena Mendizabal ordered the freedom of attorney Luis Ayllón. As a result of her action, the magistrate is sued for malfeasance by the attorneys from the Chuquisaca governorship.

- Pinto Case. On 28 May 2012, Senator Roger Pinto decides to seek refuge at Brazilian embassy. Eleven days later, Brazil gives him green light and grants him political asylum, but Bolivia never gives him necessary safe passage to depart.
- Ribera Case. On 19 June of 2012, Councilwoman Daguimar Ribera from Guayamerin is assassinated by three shots. Weeks before, Ribera started 4 suits against the town's Mayor, Alexander Guzman, for nepotism and misappropriation of public funds.[130]

The same institution reports that "as far as the persecution's axis due to political motivation, it is established that during the four month period encompassing September through December of 2012, the media reports the occurrence of at least 22 cases."[131]

If we could have reports of this kind, year by year since Evo Morales came to power, we could substantiate cases of persecution, deaths, and human rights' violations by the hundreds.

The permanent violations produced by the Coca Leaf Harvesters' Union president Evo Morales, before he came to the presidency, ought to be a motive for another similar analysis. Given that as the top leader of harvesters of the illicit coca leaf, starting in the decade of the nineties, there

---

130. El Día newspaper. Santa Cruz, 21 January of 2013.

131. New Democracy Foundation, Cited Report, Page 8.

wasn't a single year that went by without Evo Morales caus-
ing roadway blockades, marches, deaths, massacres, confrontations, without regard as to who the President, or minister
fulfilling democratic functions were.

CHAPTER 5

How to regain democracy

Under the conditions now offered by the objective reality of Bolivia, it is a national must to recover democracy. Democracy's situation, as shown by the brief description in this book of what is transpiring, is very adverse.

With all power concentrated in the hands of the president, without any possibility of the applicability of the law, with the absolute control over the force, with an organized and internationalized repressive system in-place, with the media subjected, or at the very least restricted, with the citizenry in general living under an environment of fear, with the control over international relationships and of the important players of this same project throughout the hemisphere, hope would seem to be dwindling.

History shows, however, that Bolivia and other countries have overcome similar situations although at the expense of much effort and sacrifice and those dictatorial regimes are not eternal. Dictatorships fight criminally to keep themselves in power, but end up defeated by the power of liberty and the people.

Following are some suggestions of how we Bolivians can recover democracy in our country and defeat the XXI century dictatorship in Bolivia.

5.1. Call things by their name

Following the denomination coined by the pioneer Osvaldo Hurtado,[132] it becomes fundamental to start calling Evo Morales' government by its name, by what it is: A dictatorship.

It is unfathomable for the hemisphere and the world to continue recognizing and treating Morales as a democratic president and his government as a democracy, when –as we have shown it in this book- in Bolivia today none of the essential social elements of democracy, as outlined in the Interamerican Democratic Charter, are adhered to.

If we Bolivians, in and out of the country, and friends of democracy and Bolivia in the Americas and the world, in our daily lives, in our jobs, in the media, in the comments made, in the streets, in social gatherings, in academia, in speeches, in interviews, in short; in everything we do in our daily lives, tell people that Bolivia today is under a dictatorship and that its president is a dictator, we will promote a debate that will force the chieftain and his government to

132. Hurtado, Osvaldo. XXI Century Dictatorships.

drop the façade and reveal itself, when confronted with overwhelming proof of its abuses and impositions.

Along this way, it won't be long before our country and others who are victims of this same dictatorial process, will be the subject of scrutiny and verification of evidence that in the hands of anyone unbiased person, or institution, shall show that we have affirmed herein.

5.2. The indispensable unity of the opposition

Given the consolidation of Morales' dictatorship and his decision to get reelected for a third time through electoral fraud that he has already begun to implement, beyond ideological or programmatic positions, the opposition's unity is indispensable in order to show one sole political opposition block in next elections, join forces, but above it all, minimize the deception of democracy and make evident the weaknesses of the regime.

In elections, Evo Morales can be defeated by any candidate, if there is only one political opposition's coalition.

The Chilean historical model of cooperation to defeat the dictator of their country and then govern successfully is a great example. A more recent example is the Table of Unity of Venezuela that is still struggling, with great difficulty, and that has practically won in the last elections over the candi-

date from the XXI century socialism in that country where
Maduro is illegally and illegitimately in the presidency.

To confront a dictatorship, political parties' or personal differences are meaningless and bear no weight, because
these are a central element of the totalitarian regime, in order to avoid defeat. Dictatorships promote and foster the
opposition's split, either through real confrontations, false
alliances, or through implanting fake oppositors who are
covert operators from the government and who can do just
about anything, even fake confrontations with the government and controlled offenses of the Chieftain, but who never conform a solid political opposition block, or be a part of
an effort for unity for elections.

With that in mind, the electoral process that has already
started in Bolivia, will be useful to show us who the real oppositors are, and who use that position to continue to benefit themselves from the collateral rewards that the dictatorship grants to those who help it. The sad thing, however, is
that we will know this only after Morales has reelected himself and surely —for the theatrical façade to be complete—
when he conducts a purge of all who have helped him, as
what has already happened in several cases.

When attempting to defeat and remove a dictatorship,
violence must be avoided. Violence is not a successful means
because dictators have the expertise and the monopoly, in
general, of the violence. Violent or desperate acts only
strengthen and help their propaganda apparatus to pres-

ent them as the victims and as more democrats. This is why, in many cases seen in history, when there were violent acts against dictatorships, they were situations promoted and even funded by the very dictatorships to rid themselves of impulsive and/or courageous political adversaries.

5.3. Regain the capability to complain

Despite the lack of institutionalism, despite the lack of guarantees and the environment of threats in which the Bolivian population live, it is important to regain the capability to complain. Many of the abuses by the dictator Evo Morales have been either prevented or even revoked by the timely and well disseminated complaints from honest citizens.

The social, political, civic, religious, military, peasantry, regional, union, leadership cannot stop complaining against those acts that violate their rights and freedoms. Asking, whenever necessary, for the verification of facts and processes, showing the abuse by the president and his government, are means of erosion of power that no regime can withstand. Either progressively deteriorates it or it has to resort to the repression, which in-turn weakens it quicker.

One must renounce the prudent silence that can become an accomplice and when the reach of repression is greater, one must use people outside of the country to be able to file a well documented complaint, thus protecting the local actors.

The technological revolution that we now live in the world through the internet, the social networks, and communications in real time, are making the life of dictatorships shorter and are revealing their abuses.

5.4. Awakening the solidarity from democracies all over the world

One of the issues that call our attention and that people, rightfully, ask about is why America's and the world's democracies tolerate, allow, and accept XXI Century dictatorial regimes in place in Cuba, Venezuela, Bolivia, Ecuador, and Nicaragua. And why—with their silence—allow their growth and constant attempts to add new countries to such an undesirable list.

There are several reasons, but the two most important ones in my mind set are; politics, and business. Political reasons have to do with the fact that countries of XXI Century socialism with the great outpouring of money made by Chavez for approximately 13 years and with the discretionary management of Venezuelan oil, were able to garnish enough international support to form a support group of reciprocal assistance, blockade, or protection. The business' reasons are the credit—again with Chavez dolling out the money—to countries or governments with urgencies, the commercial exchange, the credit sales of Venezuelan oil to like countries of Petrocaribe, or investment interests, in such a way that democratic governments end up being very tolerant and take refuge in the flawed reasoning that dictators "win elections and have popular support."

If, however, the violations of human rights, freedom of the press, freedom of expression are permanently shown to the international public opinion, if the abuse and outrage that has been summarily described in this book is documented and shown; if we disseminate the fact that dictatorships do not abide by some or none of the fundamental elements of democracy, we will be able to change or unsettle the comfort of tolerant states or indifferent democratic governments, and effect change and turn them to the defense of democracy.

Latin America's democratic countries must understand that the existence of XXI Century dictatorships is a threat against them and their institutional stability. In Bolivia, because this was not fully understood, democratic governments tolerated for years a relationship with the Castrist dictatorship. We committed the sin of omission, omitting the permanent violations the Castrist dictatorship had committed and continues to commit. We did not complain, nor condemn, in a timely fashion the abuses and outrage and then the same thing happened with those of Chavez's in Venezuela. This way we were easy prey for their then covert undertaking that has taken us to where we are at today.

It is a fact that cannot be hidden that from the first appearance of the ALBA, or XXI Century Socialism, the level of conflict throughout Latin-America has exponentially grown because logically, in most cases, it is promoted and funded by the project to expand the increase in non-democratic states.

5.5. Let's accept that we have lost democracy

The regaining of democracy in Bolivia and in countries occupied by the XXI Century Socialism's transnational project ALBA or "Bolivarian" will not be neither fast, nor easy, but we must start by acknowledging that we have a very serious problem, that we have lost democracy.

Faced with the objective reality shown by the referenced sources in this book, we are confronting the harsh reality of acknowledging that the situation is adverse and that perhaps too much time has passed in which Bolivian citizens have tolerated and endured the exercise of power in a totalitarian way such as the President of the Plurinational State exercises it.

Tolerance mixed with the illusion that abuse will soon end, has even gotten us to allow the replacement of the constitution, the change of the name of the country, the end of the Republic, the utilization of the judicial as a mechanism for repression and persecution, the deinstitutionalization and deformation of the Armed Forces, the existence of politically persecuted, imprisoned, or exiled citizens, and the so many other violations and injustices that have been described herein.

As with anything, we must begin by acknowledging the problem.

It is not possible, for example, that dictator Evo Morales continues celebrating and presiding over acts to commemorate the anniversary of Bolivia's return to democracy, while he imposes on Bolivians the same or worse restrictions and violations as used to happen before 1982, when the country returned to democracy.

Each and every one of the issues addressed cases and questions made, in this book are subject to verification and can be extraordinarily expanded. The challenge remains for experts in each of the topics to trace each one of the aspects and steps of the path that Bolivia has followed toward the XXI Century Dictatorship, the characteristics and effects from it, and above it all, to contribute with ideas to regain democracy.

Regaining democracy in Bolivia and in countries occupied by the XXI Century Socialism's transnational undertaking ALBA or "Bolivarian" and from its practices of neo-communism will be neither fast, nor easy. We must begin by acknowledging and accepting that we have lost democracy, and that new dictatorships are in-place in Latin-America.

Evo Morales' regime is the XXI Century Dictatorship in Bolivia.

Annex 1

Interamerican Democratic Charter

Lima, September 11, 2001

INTER-AMERICAN DEMOCRATIC CHARTER

THE GENERAL ASSEMBLY,

CONSIDERING that the Charter of the Organization of American States recognizes that representative democracy is indispensable for the stability, peace, and development of the region, and that one of the purposes of the OAS is to promote and consolidate representative democracy, with due respect for the principle of nonintervention;

RECOGNIZING the contributions of the OAS and other regional and sub-regional mechanisms to the promotion and consolidation of democracy in the Americas;

RECALLING that the Heads of State and Government of the Americas, gathered at the Third Summit of the Americas, held from April 20 to 22, 2001 in Quebec City, adopted a democracy clause which establishes that any unconstitutional alteration or interruption of the democratic order in a state of the Hemisphere constitutes an insurmountable obstacle to the participation of that state's government in the Summits of the Americas process;

BEARING IN MIND that existing democratic provisions in regional and subregional mechanisms express the same objectives as the democracy clause adopted by the Heads of State and Government in Quebec City;

REAFFIRMING that the participatory nature of democracy in our countries in different aspects of public life contributes to the consolidation of democratic values and to freedom and solidarity in the Hemisphere;

CONSIDERING that solidarity among and cooperation between American states require the political organization of those states based on the effective exercise of representative democracy, and that economic growth and social development based on justice and equity, and democracy are interdependent and mutually reinforcing;

REAFFIRMING that the fight against poverty, and especially the elimination of extreme poverty, is essential to the promotion and consolidation of democracy and constitutes a common and shared responsibility of the American states;

BEARING IN MIND that the American Declaration on the Rights and Duties of Man and the American Convention on Human Rights contain the values and principles of liberty, equality, and social justice that are intrinsic to democracy;

REAFFIRMING that the promotion and protection of human rights is a basic prerequisite for the existence of a democratic society, and recognizing the importance of the continuous development and strengthening of the inter-American human rights system for the consolidation of democracy;

CONSIDERING that education is an effective way to promote citizens' awareness concerning their own countries and thereby achieve meaningful participation in the decision-making process, and reaffirming the importance of human resource development for a sound democratic system;

RECOGNIZING that a safe environment is essential to the integral development of the human being, which contributes to democracy and political stability;

BEARING IN MIND that the Protocol of San Salvador on Economic, Social, and Cultural Rights emphasizes the great importance of the reaffirmation, development, improvement, and protection of those rights in order to consolidate the system of representative democratic government;

RECOGNIZING that the right of workers to associate themselves freely for the defense and promotion of their interests is fundamental to the fulfillment of democratic ideals;

TAKING INTO ACCOUNT that, in the Santiago Commitment to Democracy and the Renewal of the Inter-American System, the ministers of foreign affairs expressed their determination to adopt a series of effective, timely, and expeditious procedures to ensure the promotion and defense of representative democracy, with due respect for the principle of nonintervention; and that resolution AG/RES. 1080 (XXI-O/91) therefore established a mechanism for collective action in the case of a sudden or irregular interruption of the democratic political institutional process or of the legitimate exercise of power by the democratically-elected government in any of the Organization's member states, thereby fulfilling a long-standing aspiration of the Hemisphere to be able to respond rapidly and collectively in defense of democracy;

RECALLING that, in the Declaration of Nassau [AG/DEC. 1 (XXII-O/92)], it was agreed to develop mechanisms to provide assistance, when requested by a member state, to promote, preserve, and strengthen representative democracy, in order to complement and give effect to the provisions of resolution AG/RES. 1080 (XXI-O/91);

BEARING IN MIND that, in the Declaration of Managua for the Promotion of Democracy and Development [AG/DEC. 4 (XXIII-O/93)], the member states expressed their firm belief that democracy, peace, and development are inseparable and indivisible parts of a renewed and integral vision of solidarity in the Americas; and that the ability of the Organization to help preserve and strengthen democratic structures in the region will depend on the implementation of a strategy based on the interdependence and complementarity of those values;

CONSIDERING that, in the Declaration of Managua for the Promotion of Democracy and Development, the member states expressed their conviction that the Organization's mission is not limited to the defense of democracy wherever its fundamental values and principles have collapsed, but also calls for ongoing and creative work to consolidate democracy as well as a continuing effort to prevent and anticipate the very causes of the problems that affect the democratic system of government;

BEARING IN MIND that the Ministers of Foreign Affairs of the Americas, at the thirty-first regular session of the General Assembly, held in San Jose, Costa Rica, in keeping with express instructions from the Heads of State and Government gathered at the Third Summit of the Americas, in Quebec City, accepted the base document of the Inter-American Democratic Charter and entrusted the Permanent Council of the Organization with strengthening and expanding the document, in accordance with the OAS Charter, for final adoption at a special session of the General Assembly in Lima, Peru;

RECOGNIZING that all the rights and obligations of member states under the OAS Charter represent the foundation on which democratic principles in the Hemisphere are built; and

BEARING IN MIND the progressive development of international law and the advisability of clarifying the provisions set forth in the OAS Charter and related basic instruments on the preservation and defense of democratic institutions, according to established practice,

RESOLVES:

To adopt the following:

INTER-AMERICAN DEMOCRATIC CHARTER

I
Democracy and the Inter-American System

Article 1

The peoples of the Americas have a right to democracy and their governments have an obligation to promote and defend it.

Democracy is essential for the social, political, and economic development of the peoples of the Americas.

Article 2

The effective exercise of representative democracy is the basis for the rule of law and of the constitutional regimes of the member states of the Organization of American States. Representative democracy is strengthened and deepened by permanent, ethical, and responsible participation of the citizenry within a legal framework conforming to the respective constitutional order.

Article 3

Essential elements of representative democracy include, inter alia, respect for human rights and fundamental freedoms, access to and the exercise of power in accordance with the rule of law, the holding of periodic, free, and fair elections based on secret balloting and universal suffrage as an expression of the sovereignty of the people, the pluralistic system of political parties and organizations, and the separation of powers and independence of the branches of government.

Article 4

Transparency in government activities, probity, responsible public administration on the part of governments, respect for social rights, and freedom of expression and of the press are essential components of the exercise of democracy.

The constitutional subordination of all state institutions to the legally constituted civilian authority and respect for the rule of law on the part of all institutions and sectors of society are equally essential to democracy.

Article 5

The strengthening of political parties and other political organizations is a priority for democracy. Special attention will be paid to the problems associated with the high cost of election campaigns and the establishment of a balanced and transparent system for their financing.

Article 6

It is the right and responsibility of all citizens to participate in decisions relating to their own development. This is also a necessary condition for the full and effective exercise of democracy. Promoting and fostering diverse forms of participation strengthens democracy.

II

Democracy and Human Rights

Article 7

Democracy is indispensable for the effective exercise of fundamental freedoms and human rights in their universality, indivisibility and interdependence, embodied in the respective constitutions of states and in inter-American and international human rights instruments.

Article 8

Any person or group of persons who consider that their human rights have been violated may present claims or petitions to the inter-American system for the promotion and protection of human rights in accordance with its established procedures.

Member states reaffirm their intention to strengthen the inter-American system for the protection of human rights for the consolidation of democracy in the Hemisphere.

Article 9

The elimination of all forms of discrimination, especially gender, ethnic and race discrimination, as well as diverse forms of intolerance, the promotion and protection of human rights of indigenous peoples and migrants, and respect for ethnic, cultural and religious diversity in the Americas contribute to strengthening democracy and citizen participation.

Article 10

The promotion and strengthening of democracy requires the full and effective exercise of workers' rights and the application of core labor standards, as recognized in the International Labour Organization (ILO) Declaration on Fundamental Principles and Rights at Work, and its Follow-up, adopted in 1998, as well as other related fundamental ILO conventions. Democracy is strengthened by improving standards in the workplace and enhancing the quality of life for workers in the Hemisphere.

III

Democracy, Integral Development, and Combating Poverty

Article 11

Democracy and social and economic development are interdependent and are mutually reinforcing.

Article 12

Poverty, illiteracy, and low levels of human development are factors that adversely affect the consolidation of democracy. The OAS member states are committed to adopting and implementing all those actions required to generate productive employment, reduce poverty, and eradicate extreme poverty, taking into account the different economic realities and conditions of the countries of the Hemisphere. This shared commitment regarding the problems associated with development and poverty also underscores the importance of maintaining macroeconomic equilibria and the obligation to strengthen social cohesion and democracy.

Article 13

The promotion and observance of economic, social, and cultural rights are inherently linked to integral development, equitable economic growth, and to the consolidation of democracy in the states of the Hemisphere.

Article 14

Member states agree to review periodically the actions adopted and carried out by the Organization to promote dialogue, cooperation for integral development, and the fight against poverty in the Hemisphere, and to take the appropriate measures to further these objectives.

Article 15

The exercise of democracy promotes the preservation and good stewardship of the environment. It is essential that the states of the Hemisphere implement policies and strategies to protect the environment, including application of various treaties and conventions, to achieve sustainable development for the benefit of future generations.

Article 16

Education is key to strengthening democratic institutions, promoting the development of human potential, and alleviating poverty and fostering greater understanding among our peoples. To achieve these ends, it is essential that a quality education be available to all, including girls and women, rural inhabitants, and minorities.

IV

Strengthening and Preservation of Democratic Institutions

Article 17

When the government of a member state considers that its democratic political institutional process or its legitimate exercise of power is at risk, it may request assistance from the Secretary General or the Permanent Council for the strengthening and preservation of its democratic system.

Article 18

When situations arise in a member state that may affect the development of its democratic political institutional process or the legitimate exercise of power, the Secretary General or the Permanent Council may, with prior consent of the government concerned, arrange for visits or other actions in order to analyze the situation. The Secretary General will submit a report to the Permanent Council, which will undertake a collective assessment of the situation and, where necessary, may adopt decisions for the preservation of the democratic system and its strengthening.

Article 19

Based on the principles of the Charter of the OAS and subject to its norms, and in accordance with the democracy clause contained in the Declaration of Quebec City, an unconstitutional interruption of the democratic order or an unconstitutional alteration of the constitutional regime that seriously impairs the democratic order in a member state, constitutes, while it persists, an insurmountable obstacle to its government's participation in sessions of the General Assembly, the Meeting of Consultation, the Councils of the Organization, the specialized conferences, the commissions, working groups, and other bodies of the Organization.

Article 20

In the event of an unconstitutional alteration of the constitutional regime that seriously impairs the democratic order in a member state, any member state or the Secretary General may request the immediate convocation of the Permanent Council to undertake a collective assessment of the situation and to take such decisions as it deems appropriate.

The Permanent Council, depending on the situation, may undertake the necessary diplomatic initiatives, including good offices, to foster the restoration of democracy.

If such diplomatic initiatives prove unsuccessful, or if the urgency of the situation so warrants, the Permanent Council shall immediately convene a special session of the General Assembly. The General Assembly will adopt the decisions it deems appropriate, including the undertaking of diplomatic initiatives, in accordance with the Charter of the Organization, international law, and the provisions of this Democratic Charter.

The necessary diplomatic initiatives, including good offices, to foster the restoration of democracy, will continue during the process.

Article 21

When the special session of the General Assembly determines that there has been an unconstitutional interruption of the democratic order of a member state, and that diplomatic initiatives have failed, the special session shall take the decision to suspend said member state from the exercise of its right to participate in the OAS by an affirmative vote of two thirds of the member states in accordance with the Charter of the OAS. The suspension shall take effect immediately.

The suspended member state shall continue to fulfill its obligations to the Organization, in particular its human rights obligations.

Notwithstanding the suspension of the member state, the Organization will maintain diplomatic initiatives to restore democracy in that state.

Article 22

Once the situation that led to suspension has been resolved, any member state or the Secretary General may propose to the General Assembly that suspension be lifted. This decision shall require the vote of two thirds of the member states in accordance with the OAS Charter.

V

Democracy and Electoral Observation Missions

Article 23

Member states are responsible for organizing, conducting, and ensuring free and fair electoral processes.

Member states, in the exercise of their sovereignty, may request that the Organization of American States provide advisory services or assistance for strengthening and developing their electoral institutions and processes, including sending preliminary missions for that purpose.

Article 24

The electoral observation missions shall be carried out at the request of the member state concerned. To that end, the government of that state and the Secretary General shall enter into an agreement establishing the scope and coverage of the electoral observation mission in question. The member state shall guarantee conditions of security, free access to information, and full cooperation with the electoral observation mission.

Electoral observation missions shall be carried out in accordance with the principles and norms of the OAS. The Organization shall ensure that these missions are effective and independent and shall provide them with the necessary resources for that purpose. They shall be conducted in an objective, impartial, and transparent manner and with the appropriate technical expertise.

Electoral observation missions shall present a report on their activities in a timely manner to the Permanent Council, through the General Secretariat.

Article 25

The electoral observation missions shall advise the Permanent Council, through the General Secretariat, if the necessary conditions for free and fair elections do not exist.

The Organization may, with the consent of the state concerned, send special missions with a view to creating or improving said conditions.

VI

Promotion of a Democratic Culture

Article 26

The OAS will continue to carry out programs and activities designed to promote democratic principles and practices and strengthen a democratic culture in the Hemisphere, bearing in mind that democracy is a way of life based on liberty and enhancement of economic, social, and cultural conditions for the peoples of the Americas. The OAS will consult and cooperate on an ongoing basis with member states and take into account the contributions of civil society organizations working in those fields.

Article 27

The objectives of the programs and activities will be to promote good governance, sound administration, democratic values, and the strengthening of political institutions and civil society organizations. Special attention shall be given to the development of programs and activities for the education of children and youth as a means of ensuring the continuance of democratic values, including liberty and social justice.

Article 28

States shall promote the full and equal participation of women in the political structures of their countries as a fundamental element in the promotion and exercise of a democratic culture.

Annex 2

American Declaration of the Rights and Duties of Man

AMERICAN DECLARATION OF
THE RIGHTS AND DUTIES OF MAN
(Adopted by the Ninth International Conference of American States, Bogotá, Colombia, 1948)

WHEREAS:

The American peoples have acknowledged the dignity of the individual, and their national constitutions recognize that juridical and political institutions, which regulate life in human society, have as their principal aim the protection of the essential rights of man and the creation of circumstances that will permit him to achieve spiritual and material progress and attain happiness;

The American States have on repeated occasions recognized that the essential rights of man are not derived from the fact that he is a national of a certain state, but are based upon attributes of his human personality;

The international protection of the rights of man should be the principal guide of an evolving American law;

The affirmation of essential human rights by the American States together with the guarantees given by the internal regimes of the states establish the initial system of protection considered by the American States as being suited to the present social and juridical conditions, not without a recognition on their part that they should increasingly strengthen that system in the international field as conditions become more favorable,

The Ninth International Conference of American States

AGREES:

To adopt the following

AMERICAN DECLARATION OF THE RIGHTS AND DUTIES OF MAN

Preamble

All men are born free and equal, in dignity and in rights, and, being endowed by nature with reason and conscience, they should conduct themselves as brothers one to another.

The fulfillment of duty by each individual is a prerequisite to the rights of all. Rights and duties are interrelated in every social and political activity of man. While rights exalt individual liberty, duties express the dignity of that liberty.

Duties of a juridical nature presuppose others of a moral nature which support them in principle and constitute their basis.

Inasmuch as spiritual development is the supreme end of human existence and the highest expression thereof, it is the duty of man to serve that end with all his strength and resources.

Since culture is the highest social and historical expression of that spiritual development, it is the duty of man to preserve, practice and foster culture by every means within his power.

And, since moral conduct constitutes the noblest flowering of culture, it is the duty of every man always to hold it in high respect.

CHAPTER ONE

Rights

Right to life, liberty and personal security.

Article I. Every human being has the right to life, liberty and the security of his person.

Right to equality before law.
Article II. All persons are equal before the law and have the rights and duties established in this Declaration, without distinction as to race, sex, language, creed or any other factor.

Right to religious freedom and worship.
Article III. Every person has the right freely to profess a religious faith, and to manifest and practice it both in public and in private.

Right to freedom of investigation, opinion, expression and dissemination.
Article IV. Every person has the right to freedom of investigation, of opinion, and of the expression and dissemination of ideas, by any medium whatsoever.

Right to protection of honor, personal reputation, and private and family life.
Article V. Every person has the right to the protection of the law against abusive attacks upon his honor, his reputation, and his private and family life.

Right to a family and to protection thereof.
Article VI. Every person has the right to establish a family, the basic element of society, and to receive protection therefore.

Right to protection for mothers and children.
Article VII. All women, during pregnancy and the nursing period, and all children have the right to special protection, care and aid.

Right to residence and movement.

Article VIII. Every person has the right to fix his residence within the territory of the state of which he is a national, to move about freely within such territory, and not to leave it except by his own will.

Right to inviolability of the home.
Article IX. Every person has the right to the inviolability of his home.

Right to the inviolability and transmission of correspondence.
Article X. Every person has the right to the inviolability and transmission of his correspondence.

Right to the preservation of health and to well-being.
Article XI. Every person has the right to the preservation of his health through sanitary and social measures relating to food, clothing, housing and medical care, to the extent permitted by public and community resources.

Right to education.
Article XII. Every person has the right to an education, which should be based on the principles of liberty, morality and human solidarity.
Likewise every person has the right to an education that will prepare him to attain a decent life, to raise his standard of living, and to be a useful member of society.
The right to an education includes the right to equality of opportunity in every case, in accordance with natural talents, merit and the desire to utilize the resources that the state or the community is in a position to provide.
Every person has the right to receive, free, at least a primary education.

Right to the benefits of culture.
Article XIII. Every person has the right to take part in the cultural life of the community, to enjoy the arts, and to participate in the benefits that result from intellectual progress, especially scientific discoveries.

He likewise has the right to the protection of his moral and material interests as regards his inventions or any literary, scientific or artistic works of which he is the author.

Right to work and to fair remuneration.
Article XIV. Every person has the right to work, under proper conditions, and to follow his vocation freely, insofar as existing conditions of employment permit.

Every person who works has the right to receive such remuneration as will, in proportion to his capacity and skill, assure him a standard of living suitable for himself and for his family.

Right to leisure time and to the use thereof.
Article XV. Every person has the right to leisure time, to wholesome recreation, and to the opportunity for advantageous use of his free time to his spiritual, cultural and physical benefit.

Right to social security.
Article XVI. Every person has the right to social security which will protect him from the consequences of unemployment, old age, and any disabilities arising from causes beyond his control that make it physically or mentally impossible for him to earn a living.

Right to recognition of juridical personality and civil rights.
Article XVII. Every person has the right to be recognized everywhere as a person having rights and obligations, and to enjoy the basic civil rights.

Right to a fair trial.
Article XVIII. Every person may resort to the courts to ensure respect for his legal rights. There should likewise be available to him a simple, brief procedure whereby the courts will protect him from acts of authority that, to his prejudice, violate any fundamental constitutional rights.

Right to nationality.

Article XIX. Every person has the right to the nationality to which he is entitled by law and to change it, if he so wishes, for the nationality of any other country that is willing to grant it to him.

Right to vote and to participate in government.
Article XX. Every person having legal capacity is entitled to participate in the government of his country, directly or through his representatives, and to take part in popular elections, which shall be by secret ballot, and shall be honest, periodic and free.

Right of assembly.
Article XXI. Every person has the right to assemble peaceably with others in a formal public meeting or an informal gathering, in connection with matters of common interest of any nature.

Right of association.
Article XXII. Every person has the right to associate with others to promote, exercise and protect his legitimate interests of a political, economic, religious, social, cultural, professional, labor union or other nature.

Right to property.
Article XXIII. Every person has a right to own such private property as meets the essential needs of decent living and helps to maintain the dignity of the individual and of the home.

Right of petition.
Article XXIV. Every person has the right to submit respectful petitions to any competent authority, for reasons of either general or private interest, or the right to obtain a prompt decision thereon.

Right of protection from arbitrary arrest.
Article XXV. No person may be deprived of his liberty except in the cases and according to the procedures established by pre-existing law.

No person may be deprived of liberty for non-fulfillment of obligations of a purely civil character.

Every individual who has been deprived of his liberty has the right to have the legality of his detention ascertained without delay by a court, and the right to be tried without undue delay or, otherwise, to be released. He also has the right to humane treatment during the time he is in custody.

Right to due process of law.
Article XXVI. Every accused person is presumed to be innocent until proved guilty.
Every person accused of an offense has the right to be given an impartial and public hearing, and to be tried by courts previously established in accordance with pre-existing laws, and not to receive cruel, infamous or unusual punishment.

Right of asylum.
Article XXVII. Every person has the right, in case of pursuit not resulting from ordinary crimes, to seek and receive asylum in foreign territory, in accordance with the laws of each country and with international agreements.

Scope of the rights of man.
Article XXVIII. The rights of man are limited by the rights of others, by the security of all, and by the just demands of the general welfare and the advancement of democracy.

CHAPTER TWO

Duties

Duties to society.
Article XXIX. It is the duty of the individual so to conduct himself in relation to others that each and every one may fully form and develop his personality.

Duties toward children and parents.

Article XXX. It is the duty of every person to aid, support, educate and protect his minor children, and it is the duty of children to honor their parents always and to aid, support and protect them when they need it.

Duty to receive instruction.

Article XXXI. It is the duty of every person to acquire at least an elementary education.

Duty to vote.

Article XXXII. It is the duty of every person to vote in the popular elections of the country of which he is a national, when he is legally capable of doing so.

Duty to obey the law.

Article XXXIII. It is the duty of every person to obey the law and other legitimate commands of the authorities of his country and those of the country in which he may be.

Duty to serve the community and the nation.

Article XXXIV. It is the duty of every able-bodied person to render whatever civil and military service his country may require for its defense and preservation, and, in case of public disaster, to render such services as may be in his power.

It is likewise his duty to hold any public office to which he may be elected by popular vote in the state of which he is a national.

Duties with respect to social security and welfare.

Article XXXV. It is the duty of every person to cooperate with the state and the community with respect to social security and welfare, in accordance with his ability and with existing circumstances.

Duty to pay taxes.

Article XXXVI. It is the duty of every person to pay the taxes established by law for the support of public services.

Duty to work.
Article XXXVII. It is the duty of every person to work, as far as his capacity and possibilities permit, in order to obtain the means of livelihood or to benefit his community.

Duty to refrain from political activities in a foreign country.
Article XXXVIII. It is the duty of every person to refrain from taking part in political activities that, according to law, are reserved exclusively to the citizens of the state in which he is an alien.

Approved at the Ninth International Conference of American States, held in Bogota, Colombia, 1948.

Annex 3

The Forced Resignation of the Constitutionally Elected President of the Republic.
Message to the National Congress.
17 October of 2003

MESSAGE TO THE NATIONAL CONGRESS

Honorable Members of Congress:

Bolivia is living crucial hours. Democracy is under siege by corporative, political, and labor union groups that do not believe in it and use it according to their own convenience.

All of this paints a picture of sedition that, under the pretext of (*sic* protesting against) the exportation of natural gas, has violated the essence of democracy, which is the respect of the verdict of the ballot boxes for the election of those who govern.

That banner has been used, rejecting dialog, to seek my resignation, attributing to me not only the responsibility of the current problems that the Republic confronts, but also the lack of solutions. If that was the case, my resignation, which today I tender for consideration by the Honorable Congress, should be enough to resolve the national problems.

Although I fervently wish this, I fear the solution is not that simple. The profound causes of this crisis compel us to a fundamental reasoning that the passions now unleashed do not allow us to reach. Time will do that for us, and entrust myself to it seeking a serene and objective balance that the circumstances of today deny us.

We Bolivians have paid a high cost in bloodshed and lots of pain to conquer and sustain democracy. Today, we know that democracy is a privilege that must be preserved to keep the unity of the Bolivian people, with liberty and dignity. The President of the Republic is a symbol of that unity, in the midst of a national diversity that ought to be a source of pride and not of conflict, or violence.

In tendering my resignation for the consideration by the National Congress, I do so with the innermost conviction that it does not merit its acceptance, because no one can remove a duly, democratically elected President through mechanisms of pressure and violence that are on the fringes of the law. This is a fateful precedent for Bolivian and continental democracy. Congress, according to attributions contained in Article 68, paragraph 4, of the constitutional charter, must decide whether to accept it or reject it. If it accepts it, the Vice-President of the Republic must assume the Presidency and finish the term of the constitutional mandate, as outlined in Article 93-11 of the fundamental charter. This is a task that Congress must live up to with the responsibility that the present time warrants.

But, it is my duty to warn that the dangers looming over our homeland remain intact: the national disintegration, the corporativist and labor union authoritarianism and the fratricidal violence. These dangers reside in the historic circumstances in which the essence of democracy has been placed in question. I pray to God that one day we will not regret and be remorseful for all of this.

Honorable Members of Congress:

I have served Bolivia with devotion and unlimited dedication. That is the greatest reward that I have been able to reach in my lifetime. I thank God for that privilege and I ask Him from the deepest and most profound part of my heart that he will guide and bless all Bolivians.

17 October of 2003

Gonzalo Sanchez de Lozada
Constitutional President of the Republic

Annex 4

Supreme Decree N^r. 27234
Amnesty Granted by Carlos Mesa

BOLIVIA'S OFFICIAL JOURNAL # 2532
SUPREME DECREE 27234

CARLOS MESA GISBERT
CONSTITUTIONAL PRESIDENT OF THE REPUBLIC

WHEREAS:

Law Nr. 2494 of 4 August of 2003, the National Citizen's Security System Law, went into effect in a context of profound social, economic, and political crisis.

The unfortunate tragic events recently lived in the country; the social movements have vehemently questioned the traditional political system that has not met the needs or aspirations of the majority of citizens.

The National Citizen's Security System Law, with regard to the modifications of the Criminal Code, has been viewed by the population as a Security Law for the transitory passing government, to suppress all social protests and silence demands for social vindication, hindering all fundamental rights of freedom of expression and collective petitions.

In paragraph 13 of the State's Constitutional Charter, Article 96, establishes as the attribution of the President of the Republic to decree amnesty for crimes against the State's security, and due to the fact that crimes against the State's security that took place during the recent social protests, are crimes catalogued as political in nature.

According to penal doctrine, political crimes are not solely defined by objective but by subjective criteria, that have to do with the motives that determined the actions that are framed within a determined penal type.

The events that took place in the month of October, when considering their characteristics and background, as far as the motives that led these acts, can be formally viewed as crimes of the type under the purview of the National Citizen's Security System Law; it becomes evident that these did not respond to a motivation to commit crimes of a penal nature, but to the contrary they were mere social protests against the constituted government.

The National Government currently has as its priority the recovery of the validity and credibility of the Democratic System, strengthening the Rule of Law, social peace, and the reconciliation amongst all Bolivians, towards which end, one of the appropriate means is the current Supreme Decree of Amnesty, framed by the State's Constitutional Charter.

IN THE COUNCIL OF MINISTERS
DECREES:

ARTICLE 1. (OBJECTIVE). The present Supreme Decree has as its objective to grant temporary amnesty for crimes under the purview of Law Nr. 2494 of 4 August of 2003, the National Citizen's Security System Law.

ARTICLE 2. (AMNESTY).
Amnesty is granted (decreed) for all crimes under the purview of Law Nr. 2494 of 4 August of 2003, the National Citizen's Security System Law, with regard to events that took place starting on the date of the applicability of the law until and up to the date this current Supreme Decree goes into effect. For cases in rural and agricultural areas outlined in Article 2 of Supreme decree Nr. 27068 of 6 June of 2003, procedures established by Law Nr. 1715 of 18 October 1996 and all regulatory provisions shall be applied.

ARTICLE 3. (PENDING PROCEEDINGS). The incumbent Vice-Minister of Justice is hereby instructed that through the Public Defender's office, all requirements be presented to all corresponding courts and tribunals, to cease any criminal proceedings, or other pending proceedings, according to what is established by the present Supreme Decree.

The incumbent Minister of Government, in the President's office has the responsibility of executing and complying with the present Supreme Decree.

Given at the Governmental Palace of the city of La Paz, on the thirty first day of the month of October of the year of 2003.

SIGNED CARLOS D. MESA GISBERT, Jorge Gumucio Granier, Interim Minister of Foreign Affairs and Cult, José Antonio Galindo Noder, Alfonso Ferrufino Valderrama, Gonzalo Arredondo Millán, Rubén Ferrufino Goitia, Interim Minister of the Treasury, Jorge Cortés Rodriguez, Jorge Urquidi Barrau, Minister of Services and Public Works and Interim Minister of Economic Development, Alvaro Rios Roca, Donato Ayma Rojas, Fernando Antezana Aranibar, Luis Fernandez Fagalde, Diego Montenegro Ernst, Robert Barbery Anaya, Justo Seoane Parapaino.

Supreme Decree Nr. 27237
Complement to the Amnesty Granted
by Carlos Mesa

SUPREME DECREE Nr. 27237

CARLOS D. MESA GISBERT
CONSTITUTION PRESIDENT OF THE REPUBLIC

WHEREAS:

Supreme Decree Nr. 27234 of 31 October of 2003 establishes temporary amnesty for crimes under the purview of Law 2494, National Citizen's Security System Law.

Article 2 of the aforementioned law, grants (decrees) amnesty for all crimes under the purview of Law 2494, with regard to events that took place starting on the date of the applicability of the law until and up to the date this current Supreme Decree goes into effect.

It is necessary to delineate the scope of Supreme Decree 27234, in the sense that the amnesty is referred solely and only to the events of social protest that occurred commencing on 5 August of 2003, the date of issuance of Law 2494, until 4 November of 2003, the date of issuance of Supreme Decree 27234.

IN COUNCIL OF MINISTERS
DECREES:

UNIQUE ARTICLE. The amnesty decreed (granted) by Article 2 of Supreme Decree Nr. 27234 of 31 October of 2003, is applicable only to those citizens whose actions would have been committed in the time frame encompassing from 5 August to 4 November of 2003, in the environment of social protests against decisions made and policies implemented by the National Government.

The incumbent Minister of Government, in the President's office is responsible for the execution and compliance with this present Supreme Decree.

Given at the Presidential Palace, in the city of La Paz, on the fourth day of the month of November of the year of two thousand and three.

SIGNED BY CARLOS D. MESA GISBERT, Juan Ignacio Siles del Valle, José Antonio Galindo Noder, Alfonso Ferrufino Valderrama, Gonzalo Arredondo Millán, Javier Gonzalo Cuevas Argote, Jorge Cortés Rodriguez, Xavier Nogales Iturri, Jorge Urquidi Barrau, Alvaro Rios Roca, Donato Ayma Rojas, Fernando Antezana Aranibar, Luis Fernandez Fagalde, Diego Montenegro Ernst, Robert Barbery Anaya, Justo Seoane Parapaino.

REFERENCE TEXT
Official Bulletin, Plurinational State of Bolivia
Reserved Rights @ 2012

Annex 6

Law 3941
Empowering Ordinary Congress to Interpret and Draft the New Constitution

LAW NR. 3941

LAW OF 21 OCTOBER OF 2008

EVO MORALES AYMA
CONSTITUTIONAL   PRESIDENT
OF THE REPUBLIC

WHEREAS, the honorable National Congress has legislated the following law

THE HONORABLE NATIONAL CONGRESS

DECREES:

ARTICLE 1. (Constitutional Framework). In conformity to what is established by Article 233 of the State's Constitutional Charter, Article 232 of the Fundamental Law is interpreted.

ARTICLE 2. (Interpretation). In application of the Republican Institutionalism, the Principle of Popular Sovereignty, the Social and Democratic Rule of Law, determined in Articles 1, 2, and 4 of the State's Constitutional Charter, establishing that it is the Responsibility of the Honorable National Congress to contribute to the constituent process and to make all necessary adjustments to the constitutional text approved by the Constituent Assembly on the basis of the popular will and national interest, by Congress' special law, approved by two thirds of the votes of members present, the scope and reach of constitutional Article 232 is interpreted as follows:
ARTICLE 232.

The total reform of the State's Constitutional Charter is the exclusive responsibility of the Constituent Assembly which will be convened by a Special Convening Law, which will indicate the manner and modality of election of constituent assembly members, to be approved by two thirds of the votes of members of the Honorable National Congress that may not be vetoed by the President of the Republic.

Once the constituent process is concluded, following receipt of the proposed constitutional text to be subjected to the consideration of the sovereign population, the Honorable National Congress may make the necessary adjustments, on the basis of popular will and national interest, by a special Congressional law approved by two thirds of the votes of its members present.

The adjustments may not affect the essence of the constituent's will.

Refer this to the Executive Branch for constitutional purposes.

Given at the Honorable National Congress' hall on the 21st day of the month of October of the year two thousand and eight.

Signed – Alvaro Marcelo Garcia Linera, Freddy Omar Fernandez Quiroga, Heriberto Lazaro.

Annex 7

Character Assassination By XXI Century Dictatorships

REPUTATION ASSASSINATION
BY XXI CENTURY DICTATORSHIPS

Carlos Sanchez Berzain*
Published in "The America's Daily"
(El Diario Las Américas)
Miami, 20 September of 2013

The strategy of persecution by dictatorships from the XXI Century Social-ism against those who they identify as their "political enemies", those indi-viduals who they want "out of the way" (political leaders, journalists, citi-zens), or whose fortune the government has an interests in (businessmen, media owners), is based on their control of the Judicial System along with laws specifically dictated for each case. The Dictator identifies the individ-ual, then accuses him/her directly, or uses a proxy to accuse the individual of grievous acts that constitute serious crimes; the individual is publicly singled out as a common criminal, and prosecutors and judges do the rest, until the individual's character (reputation) -usually remarkably successful- is converted to that of a criminal, either sent to jail or forced into exile.

This governmental policy has an essential element which can be a stand-alone mechanism when it has no way of orchestrating a legal persecution: it is the systematic use of slander, of false accusations maliciously made to cause harm, the accusation known to be false of crimes, the indictment of crimes on the victim, of infamy, disrepute, disgrace, together with mean-ness or vileness of verbal and written defamation or libel. What is referred to as " the murder of one's honor", "the execution of one's reputation", "the assassination of one's character" is nothing new, but is an essential weapon of the dictators of the XXI Century Socialism, who manage it from their position of power on behalf of the country they control, through the me-dia, international relations, forums and the Internet. They have confiscat-ed, purchased and co-opted their national communications' media, setup more than one transnational broadcasting network, implemented weekly linked transmissions and mandatory broadcasts. They have gone as far as creating "digital action commands", specialized governmental and "independent services" offices to sow the Internet with infamy, Photoshop photography, falsified data, narratives or documents with false sources. They have stable Twitter and other social networks' staffs and participants to direct and affect the news as part of their political operation's functions. It is about influencing the national and international public opinion to turn the victim into a criminal.

They no-longer have firing squads to physically shoot or kill, as in the first decades of the Castro dictatorship; their intent is to kill the "honor" and "reputation" of the individual, to disqualify him/her in his/her own country (from where they usually have to escape), to eliminate him/her in his/her relationships, prevent them from their professional, trade or business endeavors, subject them to continuous and permanent suspicion to condemn him/her without even any due process. It is the perfect and unpunished action of violating the fundamental right of "presumption of innocence" since it accomplishes the presumption of guilt. If all of this is accompanied by court records organized by *(sic* controlled) prosecutors and judges, the case is perfect because it has "proof" and can continue to haunt the victim, subjecting him/her to international search by Interpol and a request for extradition.

There are way too many cases of victims of these actions by the governments of Cuba, Venezuela, Ecuador, Bolivia; journalists charged with libel and crimes against the State just for doing their work and exercising their freedom of the press; businessmen falsely accused of financial crimes to steal their communications' media and enterprises; democratic authorities accused of deaths perpetrated by acts committed by the very same accusers in events directed to overthrow them; politicians accused of corruption due to their investigation of governmental corruption; civic leaders accused of terrorism for defending civil rights confronted by the state's terrorism; attorneys accused of crimes for exercising the right to legal defense; leaders charged with conspiracy for making complaints.

It is also an efficient means of intimidation because no one wants to be in the situation of those unfortunate individuals chosen by the XXI Century's Socialism to have their reputation and character assassinated.

* Attorney and political scientist. Director of the Interamerican Institute for Democracy.

Annex 8

They did it!

THEY DID IT!

José Gramunt de Moragas*, SJ*.
13 October of 2013

At last, they did it! They were able to wear out and exhaust the heart of Jose Maria Bakovic, the honest and competent president of the National Highway's Service. Jailed, removed from that position of trust by the intrigue of ill intended people with no soul or civic shame, they were able to end with the exhausted heart of this illustrious Bolivian.

They jailed him even though he had no fault and had not committed any crime, and without a fair sentence. They forced him to come and go, uselessly, through different courts and tribunals of the country. There was no lack of judges, prosecutors, secretaries, and forensic physicians, who –as cogs in a grinding wheel- made it possible to manipulate the ductile and malleable legal proceedings at their whim. Sometimes they would uselessly summon the accused. Some other times they forced him to travel from one city to another. Finally, and despite a report from the Judicial Medical Institute that had corroborated the frail state of Bakovic's health, he was compelled to go before a court in the city of La Paz, even though analysis and medical reports, had warned of the risks of such a travel.

These violations of the citizens' rights, as well as other judicial monstrosities were carried out knowing full well of the advanced age of the persecuted, and the frailty of his heart. These two circumstances added, it was evident they exposed the life of their gratuitous victim to great danger. Between all, including renowned politicians, they made him go through the gauntlet of the intricacies of the judicial management, yet even more muddied by the ill intentions of the executioners. The transgressors neither had the least of consideration to the financial harm inflicted upon their victim. That righteous and brave man had to be subdued through exhaustion.

But, he would not give up. He could have joined his sons in a country less marred by political perversion. He resisted; he had to demonstrate to the nation that had seen him born and raised there, his unquestionable professional and civic conduct that was an example to be emulated by all, but that had been placed in doubt by people with an obscured conscience.

Despite it all, the malicious persecution that he had been subjected to through long and sad years, he had shouldered the duty to maintain his honor very high as his most valuable patrimony that he could leave as a legacy to his family, and as an example to all who had been, and continued to be his dear friends. His Christian faith gave him the courage and hope to confront the injustice and wickedness.

Until last Saturday, day that his exhausted heart ceased to accompany the nobility and dignity of his character. He gave up his soul to God. Only to God, a fair judge, but never to transgressor and Pharisee judges.

Is this not the true?

"Spanish Jesuit priest and journalist. Graduated as a Baccalaureate from Law School at the Central University of Madrid and in Philosophy and Technology from the San Francisco de Borja University (Barcelona). Specializing in journalism and Communication's Sciences at the University of Syracuse (US) and at the Menendez Penayo University (Spain). Lives in Bolivia since 1952. The Bolivian government granted him Bolivian citizenship in 1991. He was director of Fides Radio from La Paz, belonging to the Company of Jesus, between 1960 and 1986, and cofounder and twice President of Radiophonic Schools of Bolivia (ERBOL). In 1964 he founded the Fides News Agency (ANF), the greatest and oldest one of Bolivia that he directs since then. In the decade of the 60's, he was the first correspondent from the EFE Spanish and the DPA German news agencies in Bolivia. During 1971 he directed the Hispanic American program of Vatican Radio in Rome. He is the author of the oldest opinion column of the Bolivian press "Is this not the true?" that is published since 1960 in the main newspapers of the country.

(Source: Wikipedia)